The American Academy of Chefs Cookbook

Recipes from American Academy of Chefs members

The American Academy of Chefs

Assisted by *Restaurants & Institutions* editorial staff

Restaurants & Institutions Magazine
Cahners Publishing Company
1350 E. Touhy, Box 5080
Des Plaines, Illinois 60017-5080

Library of Congress Cataloging in Publication Data
American Academy of Chefs
The American Academy of Chefs Cookbook

85-72062

Studio photography of food for soup, salad, game, pasta,
vegetable and bread sections by Bob Vuksanovich. Studio
photography of food for appetizer section courtesy of California
Olive Industry and Alaska Seafood Marketing Institute (King
Crab Div., Salmon Div.); for seafood section courtesy of National
Fisheries Institute; for poultry section courtesy of National
Turkey Federation and National Broiler Council; for beef section
courtesy of California Beef Council; for lamb section courtesy of
New Zealand Lamb; for pork section courtesy of National
Livestock and Meat Board; for dessert section courtesy of Pacific
Coast Canned Pears.

Cahners Publishing Company
Restaurants & Institutions Magazine
1350 E. Touhy, P.O. Box 5080
Des Plaines, Illinois 60017-5080

Printed in the United States of America

CONTENTS

ACKNOWLEDGEMENTS

Our gratitude goes to all of our colleagues and friends who were involved in the development of this cookbook;

To the many Academy members whose name appears with their recipes; To the people who were involved in the logistics of putting the cookbook together:

Jon Greenwalt, Cookbook Chairman

Alec Cline, Cookbook Coordinator/Editor

Rene Roncari, Chairman, Academy of Chefs

Baron Galand, National President, American Culinary Federation

And to Edgar Stocker, Heinz Johannes, Juergen Eidmann, Gerhard Grimeissen, Audrey Rogers, Hans Roth, John Kaufmann, Dean Jaramillo, Carolyn Cline and Barbara Wilson.

Also to the Restaurants & Institutions Magazine staff:

Jane Wallace, Associate Publisher/Editorial Director

Audrey Garvey, Creative Director

Nancy Ross Ryan, Senior Editor

Nancy Backas, Food Editor

Laura de Graaf, Staff Editor

Joan McLaughlin, Special Editorial Assistant

**Rene Roncari, CEC, AAC
Chairman, Academy of Chefs**

**Alec Cline, CEC, AAC
Cookbook Coordinator/Editor**

FORWARD

The American Academy of Chefs has a proud history. Since its founding in 1952, the Academy has grown in reputation and in numbers to become the honor society of the American chef, a society that represents years of knowledge and experience of this country's most magnificent chefs. What you have before you is an accumulation of that knowledge and experience.

These recipes represent the best in American cuisine and, like American culture, embodies contributions from many, many different individuals with different ideas and methods. But, as members of the Academy, all these individuals agree that culinary excellence is the ultimate goal. I hope you find hours of dining pleasure as you enjoy this remarkable collection of culinary knowledge.

Jon Greenwalt, CEC
Academy Cookbook Chairman

Jon Greenwalt, CEC, AAC
Academy Cookbook Chairman

DEDICATION

The Academy of Chefs is the honor society of the American Culinary Federation. This honor is bestowed upon chefs whose performance is uniquely outstanding in the culinary field.

The idea was conceived that we should collect selective recipes from these pretigious Academy members for a cookbook. Making this cookbook a reality has required the contributions of many chefs.

This book is dedicated to two of our forefathers: Antonin Careme, who was the original organizer of the science of classical food arrangement, culinary terminology and recording of recipes and to George August Escoffier who expanded on Careme's culinary science.

We also dedicate this book to the present chefs of our nation who practice our forefathers' sciences and to the apprentices who are the future chefs of our nation.

Baron H. Galand, CEC, AAC, President
The American Culinary Federation

Baron Galand, CEC, AAC
President, American Culinary Federation

AMERICAN ACADEMY OF CHEFS COOKBOOK

American chefs are enjoying unprecedented recognition today. They have achieved international acclaim and developed a cuisine that combines the best of classic French techniques with fresh American ingredients and a wealth of ethnic and early American influences.

The American Culinary Federation's honor society, the American Academy of Chefs, is part of the tradition of elevating the American culinary art to its deserved heights. The academy is composed of certified executive chefs, certified culinary educators and certified pastry chefs over the age of 35 who have been actively engaged in the culinary profession for at least 15 years and have been invited to join the society.

R&I proudly presents the first collection of recipes from these honored chefs. They share their favorite recipes, developed during their tenure as leading American chefs in fine-dining establishments and academia.

Spicy German pork salad depicts the talents of the honored academy chefs.

What makes a great chef?

The chef in the kitchen of the past was primarily an artistic culinary talent, concerned with developing new dishes and often using complex methods of preparation and presentation. The patron this chef served was more often than not someone who had time and money to spare. The chef's major focus was the food and its preparation.

Today a chef's focus is still food, and creativity is key, but new responsibilities have entered the profession. The chef of the '80s must be an organizer, a manager and a buyer. The chef must know about diet and nutrition, how to plan menus and kitchen layout, and be an expert in foodservice equipment.

Proper training is important, but it becomes useful only when supplemented by practical experience. A final and important responsibility of the chef is to share years of experience and mastery of culinary arts with the new crop of chefs that enter the kitchen every year.

Chefs moving ahead of tomorrow

The American Culinary Federation was incorporated in 1929 in New York City with the goals of upgrading the culinary profession and achieving professional recognition for all U.S. chefs. It is now composed of more than 130 chapters across the nation, including the Association of Military Chefs in Europe.

The federation began as a combination of three chef's groups—the Vatel Club, the Chef's Association of America and the Societe Culinaire Philanthropique—all based in New York. The national chef's association began

to thrive in 1949 with the organization of a group known as National Members, and it held the first national convention of the ACF in Washington, D.C., in 1954.

The active ACF membership today is composed of master chefs, executive chefs, chefs de cuisine, working chefs, pastry chefs, sous chefs, pastry cooks and journeyman cooks. All members subscribe to the culinarian's code of ethics. (Most chapters have associate members, auxiliaries and junior members, all without voting rights.) Industry purveyors participate in the ACF through associate memberships held by company representatives who have applied and been accepted as individual members.

Members are entitled to compete in national ACF-approved culinary shows and international culinary contests, seminars and cooking forums. Educational training programs are available for future cooks and chefs, and a continuing education program is available for active chefs.

A major breakthrough for American chefs came about in 1976 when chefs were officially recognized by the Department of Labor as professionals. The profession of chef is now entered in the Directory of Occupational Titles.

In 1952, the national board of directors developed an honor society within the American Culinary Federation called the Academy of Chefs. The academy is an integral part of the ACF and is headed by a chairman and secretary-treasurer, both elected by academy members.

There were 37 members when the academy first began. Today there are more than 700 academy members. To be a candidate for academy consideration, the person must be of exceptional professional and moral character. Candidates are nominated by local ACF chapters and must fulfill certain criteria in order to be considered for membership, including active ACF membership and certified executive chef status.

Membership is by invitation only, and new inductees must pledge themselves to uphold the academy's traditions, give of their time and knowledge to teach and inspire young persons interested in entering the culinary field, and further the aims and ambitions of those in the culinary profession.

Honorary membership is awarded to outstanding individuals who have distinguished themselves in the culinary arts through unselfish efforts.

Recommendation for honorary membership is made by the chairman and must be voted upon unanimously by the membership present at the board of directors meeting.

Academy members are constantly cooperating with local and national hotels, restaurant associations, schools, institutions, culinary expositions, and radio and television programs.

The making of a cookbook

Several years ago, the academy decided it was time to collect recipes from its membership with the purpose of publishing a cookbook. Members were solicited to send in their best recipes and a selection committee was formed to review incoming recipes and pick out the best 300 to 400 recipes.

The recipes are divided into 13 categories: appetizers, soups, salads, vegetables, pasta, beef, pork, lamb, poultry, seafood, game, bread and desserts. Recipes range from the classic such as Sweet-Sour Pork, Braised Ribs, Spaetzle, Liver Pâté and Poached Pears to more unusual dishes such as Wild Rice Soup and Swiss Potato Cake.

Academy members have written introductions to each section, including pertinent information related to the kitchen.

Uncovering the first academy cookbook with a collection of favorite recipes such as Savannah Fish Stew and Steamed Mussels served with a Rich Egg Sauce.

APPETIZERS

Appetizers, when they are at their best, set the stage for things to come: (clockwise from top) Oyster Cheese Pie, Salmon Mousse and Cooked Antipasto.

An appetizer can be defined as a small portion of food or drink served before a meal. Appetizers include a variety of food combinations that are designed to stimulate the appetite and prepare it for the meal to come. There are five basic categories of appetizers:

–Cocktails—shrimp, crabmeat, lobster, fruits and vegetables, or fruit and vegetable juices.

–Appetizer salads—antipasto, pickled herring, smoked salmon, deviled eggs, chicken livers.

–Hors d'oeuvres—Should be small enough to be eaten with the fingers, a toothpick or a small fork when served at the table. They can be hot or cold and include such foods as miniature sausages, bite-sized cheeses or meats, glazed shrimp, or various meatballs.

–Canapés—Tiny open-faced sandwiches, they should be bite size and are usually highly flavored or tangy. They can be any of the same combinations or mixes as hors d'oeuvres, but are served on a base such as bread, toast or crackers.

–Relishes—Carrot curls, scallions, stuffed olives, pickles and other non-prepared finger food.

Appetizers can be elaborate or simple. Many attractive and delicious ones are the result of an ingenious presentation of inexpensive ingredients. Not only do they add interest to the meal, they afford an opportunity to introduce colorful and refreshing foods to the menu.

—John W. Kaufmann

Oyster Cheese Pie (C. Imaz)

Ingredients	4 portions	Method
Pie shell, prepared, 9 in.	1	Sprinkle salmon evenly over bottom of shell.
Smoked salmon, minced	1 Tbsp.	
Oysters	2 cups	Drain; reserve ½ cup of the liquor. Place half of the oysters over bottom of shell.
Cream, light	1 cup	Heat in saucepan until scalded; remove from heat.
Onion slices, thin	2 oz.	
Clove	1	
Bay leaf, small	1	
Salt	to taste	
White pepper	to taste	
Celery salt	to taste	
Thyme	to taste	
Reserved oyster liquor	½ cup	Add; strain and let cool.
Eggs, large	4	Stir in sherry; pour half of the mixture into shell.
Sherry	3 Tbsp.	
Swiss cheese, grated, divided	½ cup	Sprinkle ¼ cup of the cheese over pie; top with remaining oysters. Add remaining sauce; top with remaining cheese. Bake at 350F for 30 minutes or until top is delicately brown.
Reserved oysters	1 cup	
Butter	2 Tbsp.	

Calamari Puffs (B. Cutino)

Ingredients	6 portions	Method
Squid, cleaned, finely ground	12 oz.	Mix well; let stand for 15 minutes. Roll into ½-oz. balls.
Bread crumbs, seasoned	3 oz.	
Eggs, whole	2	
Flour, all-purpose	3 oz.	Coat each ball.
Milk	1 oz.	Mix; dip each ball.
Egg	1	
Bread crumbs, seasoned	3 oz.	Coat each ball. Deep fry at 350F until golden. Drain and serve.

Cooked Antipasto   (J. Marzina)

Ingredients	8-10 portions	Method
Mushrooms, ½-in. dice	1 lb.	Cook vegetables in oil until tender.
Cauliflower, cooked, ½-in. dice	1 lb.	
Medium carrots, ½-in. dice	4	
Green bell peppers, ½-in. dice	4	
Large onions, ½-in. dice	2	
Celery rib, ½-in. dice	1	
Garlic cloves, pared, chopped	3	
Olive oil	1 cup	
Ketchup	28 oz.	Add; simmer for 10 minutes. Serve hot or cold.
Chili sauce	16 oz.	
King crab meat, chopped	1 lb.	
Tuna fish, flaked	6½ oz.	
Green olives, pitted	½ cup	
Ripe olives, pitted	½ cup	
Lemon juice	2 lemons	
Salt	1 Tbsp.	

Escargot John III   (J. Kaufmann)

Ingredients	6 portions	Method
Snails	36	Marinate in refrigerator overnight; strain; reserve marinade and snails separately.
Garlic cloves, pared, minced	6	
Cognac	6 tsp.	
Mushrooms, minced	6	Sauté. Add reserved marinade; flame; reduce.
Butter	2 Tbsp.	
Puff pastry sheet	1	Cut into 1½-in. squares; place small amount of mushroom mixture and one snail on each square; fold over. Bake at 400F for 10 minutes. Serve hot.

Salmon Mousse   (V. Karoli)

Ingredients	6 portions	Method
Salmon, fresh	1 lb., 8 oz.	Cover salmon with water. Add wine, lemon slices, onion, bay leaf, peppercorns and thyme. Simmer until salmon flakes easily. Drain; reserve 1 cup of the fish stock. Let cool; flake fish.
White wine	½ cup	
Lemon slices, unpeeled	3	
Onion, pared, chopped	1 tsp.	
Bay leaf	½	
Peppercorns	3	
Thyme	to taste	
Reserved fish stock	1 cup	Cook in double boiler, stirring, until thick and smooth.
Egg, lightly beaten	1	
Vinegar	2 Tbsp.	
Flour	1 Tbsp.	
Salt	1 tsp.	
Dry mustard	¾ tsp.	
Celery, chopped	2 Tbsp.	Add with flaked fish.
Cucumber, pared, chopped	2 Tbsp.	
Gelatin, softened in ¼ cup cold water	1 Tbsp.	
Heavy cream, whipped	½ cup	Fold in. Pour into mold; refrigerate until firm. Serve with lettuce hearts.

Swiss De Alps Pie (S. Muthofer)

Ingredients	4 portions	Method
Pastry shell, 9-in., half-baked	1	Layer broccoli, ham, tomato and cheese in pastry shell. Sprinkle onion over top; reserve.
Broccoli, blanched, drained, diced	2 oz.	
Ham or bacon, ½-in. dice	1½ oz.	
Swiss cheese, shredded	6 oz.	
Tomato, peeled, ¼-in. dice	2 Tbsp.	
Onion, pared, chopped	1 tsp.	
Milk, scalded	1 cup	Combine; pour into reserved pastry shell. Bake at 450F for 10 minutes. Reduce heat to 325F; bake for 30 to 35 minutes. Remove from oven; let stand several minutes before serving.
Eggs, lightly beaten	4	
Tarragon	1 tsp.	
Pepper	¾ tsp.	
Salt	½ tsp.	
Nutmeg	to taste	
Butter, melted	as needed	Brush pie with melted butter; sprinkle with parsley.
Parsley, freshly chopped	as needed	

Cheese Log Appetizers (K. Eid)

Ingredients	10-12 portions	Method
Sharp cheddar cheese, grated	1 lb.	Combine thoroughly with hands (if too dry, add more beer). Shape into 2-in.-diameter roll. Refrigerate until firm.
Medium cheddar cheese, grated	1 lb.	
Cream cheese, softened	8 oz.	
Sour cream	½ cup	
Pecans, chopped	½ cup	
Beer	3 Tbsp.	
Onion, pared, minced, sautéed	3 Tbsp.	
Worcestershire sauce	3 tsp.	
Garlic cloves, pared, crushed	3	
Hot pepper sauce	2 dashes	
Chili powder	as needed	Mix; sprinkle over rolling board; roll cheese log in mixture. Cut into ⅛-in. slices.
Paprika	as needed	
Pumpernickel rounds	3 doz.	Place on 2-in. pumpernickel rounds (rye rounds or puff pastry can be substituted). Decorate with pecan halves.
Pecan halves	3 doz.	

The Real Italian Antipasto (M. Di Salvo)

Ingredients	8 portions	Method
Olive oil	¼ cup	Combine for a marinade.
Parsley, chopped	1 tsp.	
Garlic cloves, pared, chopped	2	
Salt	to taste	
Pepper	to taste	
Pimentos, cut into ¼-in. strips	1 4-oz. can	Add; marinate overnight.
Prosciutto slices	16	Arrange on individual plates.
Italian salami slices	16	
Capocollo slices	8	
Fontinella cheese, sliced	1 lb.	
Olives	16	
Pepperoncini	8	
Anchovies	16	Roll anchovies around butter cubes. Place on plates.
Butter, cut into 16 ¼-in. cubes	¼ lb.	Add marinated pimentos just before serving.

Ham Spread (T. Richardson)

Ingredients	5-10 portions	Method
Ham, cooked, finely ground	1 lb.	Combine thoroughly. Place in serving bowl. Refrige-
Cream cheese	½ lb.	rate. Can be served as a dip, spread or filling.
Marsala	½ cup	
Worcestershire sauce	½ tsp.	
Dry mustard	¼ tsp.	
Cloves, ground	¼ tsp.	

Lau Laus (D. Chen)

Ingredients	20 portions	Method
Salt pork or bacon, julienne	8 oz.	Sauté.
Oil	4 oz.	
Chinese bok choy leaves, shredded	4 lb.	Add leaves and shallots; heat until leaves cook down. Add seasonings. Remove from pan; let drain.
Shallots, chopped	1 Tbsp.	
Sugar	2 tsp.	
White pepper	1 tsp.	
Salt	to taste	
Raw chicken breast, sliced	2 lb.	Combine well.
Green onions, chopped	2 bunches	
Oil	3 Tbsp.	
Lemon juice	2 Tbsp.	
Sherry	2 Tbsp.	
Cornstarch	2 Tbsp.	
Sugar	1 tsp.	
White pepper	1 tsp.	
Worcestershire sauce	1 tsp.	
Hot pepper sauce	4 dashes	
Ti leaves, washed	40 pieces	Place 2 of the ti leaves on each plate. Place some of the shredded bok choy in center; top with some of the chicken mixture. Pull ends up; tie with string. Steam for 30 minutes or until done. Cut top of ti leaves to serve.

Poached Egg Green Mountain
(J. Nargi)

Ingredients	1 portion	Method
English muffin, toasted	1	Place bacon on muffin.
Bacon strips, cooked	2 or 3	
Spinach, chopped	½ cup	Sauté; spoon over bacon.
Olive oil	1 Tbsp.	
Garlic clove, pared, crushed	1	
Egg, poached	1	Place egg on spinach mixture; top with cheese. Heat in broiler or hot oven until cheese is melted. Sprinkle generously with chopped parsley. Serve immediately.
American cheese slice	1	
Parsley, chopped	1 tsp.	

Steak Tartare with Lemon
(H. Warren)

Ingredients	4 portions	Method
Onion, pared, minced	⅓ cup	Combine thoroughly in large mixing bowl; transfer to small bowl.
Parsley, fresh, coarsely chopped	3 Tbsp.	
Green onions, tops only, coarsely chopped	2 Tbsp.	
Capers, coarsely chopped	2 Tbsp.	
Worcestershire sauce	1 Tbsp.	
Dijon-style mustard	1 Tbsp.	
Horseradish, grated	2 tsp.	
Anchovy fillets, minced	2	
Garlic clove, pared, crushed	½	
Hot pepper sauce	to taste	
Sirloin steak or tenderloin, freshly ground, chilled	1½ lb.	Place meat in large bowl; add egg; mix well.
Egg	1	
Fresh lemon juice	¼ cup	Add; mix well. Combine thoroughly with vegetable mixture. Taste and adjust seasonings.
Lemon rind, finely grated	½ tsp.	
Pumpernickel bread slices, square, extra thin	4	Lightly spread butter on bread. Place 1 slice of bread on each chilled plate. Top with steak mixture. Sprinkle tops with chopped parsley. Garnish plates with clusters of olives, radishes and lemon quarters.
Butter, unsalted	as needed	
Parsley, chopped	as needed	

Fresh Crab Hors D'Oeuvre
(K. Eid)

Ingredients	10-12 portions	Method
Cheddar cheese, grated	8 oz.	Soften in microwave oven; beat for 3 minutes.
Butter	4 oz.	
Parmesan cheese, grated	4 oz.	Add.
Onion, pared, chopped, sautéed	4 Tbsp.	
Worcestershire sauce	1 Tbsp.	
Salt	to taste	
Pepper	to taste	
Crab meat, fresh, chopped small	1 lb.	Fold in; combine well.
French bread, cut into bite-size pieces, toasted	as needed	Serve on toasted bread. Heat in broiler before serving.

Escargot de Stowe   (A. Flory)

Ingredients	12 portions	Method
Large cucumbers Butter Oil	6 2 oz. 4 Tbsp.	Pare cucumbers; score lengthwise with fork. Trim and discard ends. Cut into 8 1-in.-thick pieces; hollow out with melon baller, leaving bottom. Sauté in butter and oil until lightly glazed. Season as desired. Cover; reserve.
Oil Shallots, minced	1 Tbsp. 2 Tbsp.	Sauté until shallots are lightly glazed.
Walnuts, minced	2 Tbsp.	Add.
Butter, room temperature	½ lb.	Stir shallots and nuts into butter with fork.
Anise-flavored liqueur Watercress, chopped Parsley, chopped Medium garlic cloves, pared, crushed Black pepper, fresh	2 Tbsp. 2 Tbsp. 1 Tbsp. 2 to taste	Add.
Large snails	48	Heat some of the snail butter in sauté pan until melted. Add snails; sauté until hot (do not overcook).
Brandy Glace de viande or brown sauce	2 Tbsp. 1 Tbsp.	Deglaze pan; reserve hot. Place 1 snail in each reserved cucumber rondelle; place on broiler pan. Top with remaining snail butter; heat in broiler until brown. Serve immediately. Serve with reserved hot snail butter.

Tureen of Lobster Pâté   (B. Cutino)

Ingredients	6 portions	Method
Lobster meat Heavy cream Egg yolks Lemon juice Butter, melted Salt White pepper Nutmeg	12 oz. 4 oz. 2 1 Tbsp. ½ oz. ½ tsp. ½ tsp. ¼ tsp.	Purée in food processor. Place 12-x-14-in. piece of buttered waxed paper over 12-x-14-in. piece of aluminum foil. Place mixture in 6-x-12-in. strip on paper.
Lobster meat	4 oz.	Place lengthwise in center of mixture. Tightly roll up foil; twist ends. Place roll on rack in water bath; bake at 350F for 45 minutes. Remove; refrigerate for 6 hours. Unroll. Slice into 2-in. portions. Serve with lemon-dill, mayonnaise or champagne aspic.

Swiss Cheese Puffs   (C. Richter)

Ingredients	4 portions	Method
Swiss cheese, shredded Large egg white Kirschwasser	8 oz. 1 1 tsp.	Combine thoroughly. Shape into ½-oz. balls about the size of small walnuts.
Oil	as needed	Heat in oil at 375F until golden. Serve immediately on folded napkin.

Provençale Cheese (F. Buck)

Ingredients	4 portions	Method
Brie, Camembert, feta or Coulommiers cheese	10 oz.	Pierce cheese on both sides with fork or skewer. Place in crockpot or glass jar.
Olive oil	1 pt.	Combine; pour over cheese. Refrigerate covered for at least 1 week, turning cheese occasionally. To serve, wrap in grape leaves.
Shallot, pared, sliced	1	
Sambal Oelek	1 tsp.	
Rosemary, fresh	1 Tbsp., 1 tsp.	
Thyme	1 Tbsp., ½ tsp.	
Black peppercorns, cracked	2 tsp.	
Bay leaves	2	

Liver Pâté a la John's (J. Kosec)

Ingredients	8-10 portions	Method
Pork fat or bacon slices	12-15	Arrange in pan so ends hang over edge to half the depth of the pan. Cover pan evenly; set aside.
Chicken livers, fresh	1 lb.	Drain livers; purée with anchovies in blender or food processor.
Anchovy fillets	3	
Eggs	6	Mix; add, blending well.
Flour	1 cup	
Light cream	1 cup	Add.
White pepper	½ tsp.	Slowly add; mix well.
Allspice	½ tsp.	
Salt	½ tsp.	
Black pepper	to taste	
Brandy	½ cup	Add; mix until just blended. Pour into bacon-lined mold; cover. Top with overhanging strips; place in water bath with water half the depth of mold. Bake at 225F for 2 to 2½ hours.
Pistachios or almonds	4 oz.	

Spinach-Cheese Puff Triangles (S. Nicas)

Ingredients	10 4-piece servings	Method
Onion, pared, minced	1 large	Sauté onion in oil until transparent. Add spinach; let cool.
Olive oil	¼ cup	
Spinach leaves, cleaned, stems trimmed, finely chopped	1¼ lb.	
Feta cheese, drained, finely crumbled	1 lb.	Add, stirring to evaporate water.
Eggs, beaten	6	Add; taste and adjust seasonings.
Chicken or veal velouté	1 cup	
White peppercorns, freshly ground	1 tsp.	
Phyllo pastry sheets	1 lb.	Brush 2 of the phyllo sheets at a time with melted butter (keep remaining sheets covered). Stack the 2 sheets. Cut into 3-in. strips. Place 1 Tbsp. of the filling at one end of each strip; fold like a flag. Brush each triangle with melted butter. Bake at 425F for 15 minutes or until puffed and golden.
Butter, melted	1 lb.	

Cheese Spread (L. Schaeli)

Ingredients	4-6 portions	Method
Blue cheese or Roquefort, diced small	3 oz.	Combine, using two forks, until mixture is a smooth paste. Serve with stone ground wheat crackers or as celery stuffing.
Cream cheese	3 oz.	
Unsalted butter	2 oz.	
Heavy cream	¼ cup, 1 Tbsp.	
Brandy	3 Tbsp.	
Dijon-style mustard	1 tsp.	
Worcestershire sauce	to taste	
Hot pepper sauce	to taste	

Fish Roe Dip (A. Pefanis)

Ingredients	3-4 portions	Method
Carp roe	3 oz.	Combine.
Small onion, pared, minced	1	
Olive oil	1 to 2 cups	Add a little of the oil; beat thoroughly until mixture is smooth paste.
White bread, trimmed	4 or 5 slices	Moisten bread; squeeze out excess moisture.
Water	as needed	
Lemons, juice of	2 or 3	Continue beating carp roe mixture, alternately adding small pieces of bread, olive oil and lemon juice. Beat until cream-colored. Serve as a dip with crackers or spread on toast.

Tunny Hors D'Oeuvre Pâté (T. Richardson)

Ingredients	4-10 portions	Method
Tuna fish (if in water, drain well), finely ground	1 lb.	Combine thoroughly; place in serving bowl. Refrigerate. Use as a dip, spread or filling.
Cream cheese	½ lb.	
Chablis	½ cup	
Fresh lemon juice	½ Tbsp.	
Salt	to taste	
White pepper	to taste	

Teriyaki Pork Cubes (M. Piccinino)

Ingredients	4-6 portions	Method
Water	12 oz.	Combine for marinade.
Soy sauce	6 oz.	
Lime, cut in half	1	
Garlic clove, pared, minced	1	
Brown sugar	1 oz.	
Ginger, ground	to taste	
Pork, 1-in. cubes	1 lb.	Marinate in refrigerator for at least 3 days. Drain.
Flour	as needed	Coat pork cubes. Deep-fry at 300F until golden. Serve hot with dipping sauces.

Swiss Cheese Tartelettes   **(B. Urban)**

Ingredients	8 portions	Method
Puff pastry	8 oz.	Roll out puff pastry to ⅛-in.-thick sheet. Cut circles to fit tart molds; line tart molds with circles.
Milk	1 cup	Combine; fill molds. Bake at 350F for 25 minutes. Serve hot.
Gruyère cheese, grated	3 oz.	
Emmenthaler cheese, grated	3 oz.	
Eggs	2	
White pepper	to taste	
Nutmeg	to taste	

Quiche Lorraine   **(F. Nikodemus)**

Ingredients	10 portions	Method
Flour	4 cups	Mix with hands until smooth.
Butter, softened	6 oz.	
Salt	½ tsp.	
Eggs	2	Add; mix until dough becomes firm. Roll on floured board to ⅛-in. thickness to fit 9-in. pie plate (makes three 9-in. pie shells). Trim edges. Refrigerate for 30 minutes.
Water, cold	½ cup	
Crab meat, chopped	6 oz.	Sprinkle over bottom of shell.
Swiss cheese, diced	¼ cup	
Light cream	1½ cups	Combine thoroughly at high speed in blender or food processor. Pour over crab meat and cheese. Bake at 350F for about 30 minutes or until pie is firm and golden. Serve warm.
Eggs	5	
Chives, chervil and parsley, chopped	1 Tbsp.	
Salt	to taste	
White pepper	to taste	
Nutmeg	to taste	

SOUPS

Nothing tells as much about a chef's creativity as soup: (clockwise from top) Soup of Wild Duckling, Minnesota Wild Rice Soup and Iced Cold Senegalese Soup.

Soup is good food, and in most cases, good soups are made from good stock. Stock is made merely by leaching out the nutrients by simmering bones, meat scraps, fowl, knucklebones and fish heads with pieces and bits of celery, onions, carrots, tomatoes, mushrooms and most any type of vegetable with exception of lettuce. These ingredients should be started in cold water, then simmered for about three hours. The stock is then strained with only the liquid to be used as soup base.

There are 10 basic soups:

–Bouillon—concentrated stock.
–Consommé—a clarified double-strength stock.
–Broth—a clear liquid made by simmering fish, meats, fowl and vegetables.
–Jellied soup—made by simmering gelatins and knucklebones or by adding gelatin to consommé.
–Vegetable soup—made by cooking a variety of vegetables in stock.
–Purées—soups made of puréed beans, peas or fresh vegetables, especially high-starch vegetables.

–Cream soups—a soup made with cream or milk thickened with equal amounts of butter and flour or egg yolks.
–Bisques—a shellfish-base cream soup.
–Chowder—a thick fish or clam base cream soup, where diced vegetables are added.
–Fruit or squash—mostly made with cream or sour cream and berries, pumpkin, cantaloupe or fruits and squashes. Served cold.

Soups that are to be served hot should be served very hot, and cold soup should be served chilled. **—Jon Greenwalt**

Iced Cold Senegalese Soup   (J. Lubinski)

Ingredients	6 portions	Method
Medium onion, pared, chopped	1	Sauté in large saucepan for 5 minutes. Remove from heat.
Carrot, pared, sliced	1	
Celery rib, sliced	1	
Garlic cloves, pared, chopped	3	
Butter	3 Tbsp.	
Curry powder	2 Tbsp.	Add; stir well.
Flour	2 Tbsp.	
Tomato paste	1 Tbsp.	Add; heat, stirring constantly, to boiling.
Cloves	6	Add; simmer for 30 minutes or until reduced by ⅔. Strain; let cool.
Small cinnamon stick	1	
Heavy cream	1½ cups	Add; refrigerate. Serve very cold.
Light chicken meat, cooked, diced	½ cup	

Minnesota Wild Rice Soup   (W. Lyman)

Ingredients	6-8 portions	Method
Wild rice, rinsed, drained	¼ cup	Cook rice in chicken stock, covered, over medium heat for about 45 minutes or until tender.
Chicken stock	1 qt.	
Onion, pared, diced	½ cup	While rice is cooking, sauté until onion is transparent.
Celery, diced	¼ cup	
Carrot, pared, diced	¼ cup	
Butter	¼ cup	
Flour	½ cup	Add; cook, stirring, over medium heat for 2 to 3 minutes. Add cooked wild rice and chicken stock while stirring.
Almonds, slivered	2 Tbsp.	Add; simmer for 10 to 15 minutes.
Ham, diced	¼ cup	
Salt	½ tsp.	
White pepper	⅛ tsp.	
Light cream	2 cups	Add; heat thoroughly; taste and adjust seasonings.

Soup of Wild Duckling
(W. Daffinger)

Ingredients	12 portions	Method
Wild duckling, cleaned, cut into pieces	1	Brown duckling in bacon fat.
Bacon fat	3 Tbsp.	
Carrot, pared, chopped	1	Add; sauté.
Celery rib, chopped	1	
Parsley root, pared, chopped	1	
Leek, white part only, chopped	1	
Medium onion, pared, chopped	½	
Garlic cloves, pared, minced	2	
Tomato purée	¼ cup	Add; heat for 3 minutes.
Chicken stock	3¼ qt.	Add; heat to boiling.
Lentils, washed, soaked	1 lb.	
Juniper berries, crushed	1 tsp.	Add; simmer until lentils and duckling pieces are done. Strain; remove meat from bones. Cut into strips; reserve for garnish.
White peppercorns, crushed	1 tsp.	
Bay leaves	2	
Cloves	3	
Rosemary leaves	¼ tsp.	
Salt	to taste	
Dry sherry	1 cup	Add; taste and adjust seasonings; serve hot.

Escarole Soup
(K. Muller)

Ingredients	6-8 portions	Method
Chicken fat or butter	1 oz.	Melt in a saucepan.
Carrots, pared, chopped	4 oz.	Add; sauté for several minutes.
Onion, pared, chopped	2 oz.	
Celery, chopped	2 oz.	
Escarole, rinsed, cut into 1-in. pieces	1 head	Sauté for several minutes.
Chicken or veal stock	2 qt.	Add; heat to simmering.
Bay leaf	1	
Pepper	⅛ tsp.	
Salt	to taste	
Bread slice	1	Soak bread in milk.
Milk	2 Tbsp.	
Egg	1	Add to bread; mix well. Form into balls the size of small cherries; drop into simmering soup. Simmer until meatballs are cooked and vegetables are tender but firm.
Cheese, grated	1 Tbsp.	
Salt	½ tsp.	
Parsley, chopped	½ tsp.	
Garlic clove, pared, minced	¼	
Basil, minced	¼ tsp.	
Thyme, minced	¼ tsp.	

Carrot and Orange Soup   (J. Douglas)

Ingredients	8-10 portions	Method
Frozen orange concentrate	1 cup	Place in soup pot.
Chicken stock	1 gal.	Add; heat to boiling; simmer for 1 hour.
Carrots, pared, puréed	9 oz.	
Orange, zest grated, reserved for garnish	½	
Onion, pared, puréed	¼ cup	
Clove	1	
Garlic clove, pared, crushed	½	
Sugar	1½ oz.	Add; taste and adjust seasonings.
Salt	to taste	
White pepper	to taste	
Cornstarch, dry	⅔ cup	Mix with enough water to form a paste. Add enough of the cornstarch mixture until proper consistency is achieved. Strain as much of the pulp as possible through china cap.
Cold water	as needed	
Heavy cream	1 pt.	Add with reserved zest. Taste and adjust seasonings.
Egg yolks	3	
Orange-flavored liqueur	to taste	

Crab Cioppino   (A. Davis)

Ingredients	8 portions	Method
Olive oil	¼ cup	Sauté until tender.
Onions, pared, chopped, dry	2 cups	
Celery, thinly sliced	1 cup	
Mushrooms, fresh, sliced	1 cup	
Garlic cloves, pared, crushed	2 Tbsp.	
Hungarian paprika	2 tsp.	Add; stir for several minutes.
Whole rosemary	2 tsp.	
Salt	2 tsp.	
Whole spice	1 tsp.	
Sweet basil	1 tsp.	
Oregano	1 tsp.	
Pepper	½ tsp.	
Dill seed	¼ tsp.	
Bay leaves, crushed	3	
Tomatoes, stewed, diced	1 qt.	Add; heat to boiling. Reduce heat; simmer for at least 1 hour.
Water	1 qt.	
Dry red wine	1 cup	
Mushrooms, chopped, dry	½ cup	
Tomato paste	½ cup	
Dungeness crabs, 3 lb. each	4	Meanwhile, crack and clean crabs; reserve all fat from crabs. Cut lobster tail with shell on into 1-in. slices.
Lobster tail, 14 to 16 oz.	1	
Raw clams, in shell	2 lb.	When sauce has simmered for at least 1 hour, add with crab, reserved crab fat and lobster tail. Simmer until clams open. Serve in large bowls.
Shrimp, 16 ct., in shell	1 lb.	
Parsley, chopped	½ cup	Garnish.

Rhode Island Quahog Chowder (S. Inonog)

Ingredients	15 portions	Method
Onion, pared, chopped Celery, chopped Butter	1 cup 1 cup 4 Tbsp.	Sauté until onion is translucent.
Quahogs, freshly shucked	3 qt.	Measure quahogs after they are shucked. Grind through meat grinder, using ½-in. plate, or chop into ½-in. pieces.
Water Clam juice Potatoes, pared, diced Salt Black pepper Marjoram	1½ qt. 1 pt. 6½ cups 2 tsp. ½ tsp. ¼ tsp.	Combine with onion mixture and quahogs; simmer for 35 to 40 minutes or until potatoes are very tender.

Catalan Vegetable Soup (M. Loritts)

Ingredients	8 portions	Method
Onions, pared, chopped Leeks, white part only, washed, chopped Olive oil Butter, sweet	2 2 3 Tbsp. 2 Tbsp.	Sauté onions and leeks in olive oil and butter until onions are soft.
Celery ribs, chopped Tomatoes, ripe, peeled, diced	2 3	Add; cook until tomatoes are reduced and very soft.
Beef bouillon Medium potatoes, pared, raw, dried Dry white wine	6 cups 2 ⅓ cup	Add; cook for 30 minutes or until potatoes are very soft.
Parsley, minced	1 tsp.	Serve or purée in blender or food processor. Garnish with minced parsley.

Brazilian Peanut Soup (H. Jordi)

Ingredients	10-12 portions	Method
Butter	¾ cup	Melt in 3-qt. saucepan.
Celery, chopped Medium onions, pared, chopped	1 cup 2	Add; sauté until soft.
Flour	½ cup	Add; stir well.
Chicken stock, heated	2 qt.	Add; stir well; simmer over low heat for 20-30 minutes.
Salt White pepper Nutmeg	to taste to taste to taste	Add.
Chunky peanut butter	2 cups	Add; stir until completely dissolved.
Heavy cream	1 cup	Add. Tasté and adjust seasonings. Serve with cinnamon croutons.

Viennese Goulash Soup

Ingredients	20 portions	Method
Vegetable oil	⅓ cup	Sauté until meat is light brown.
Beef, cut into ¼-in. cubes	1 lb.	
Onions, pared, diced	1 lb.	Add; sauté until onions are translucent.
Celery, diced	½ cup	
Carrots, pared, diced	⅓ cup	
Beef stock	5 qt.	Add; cook until potatoes are done.
Potatoes, pared, diced	1 lb.	
Tomato purée	1½ cups	
Paprika	1 Tbsp.	
Garlic powder	½ tsp.	
Marjoram	½ tsp.	
Large bay leaves	2	
Shortening	6 oz.	Mix; heat; whip into soup. Heat to boiling. Taste and adjust seasonings.
Flour	6 oz.	

Black Bean Soup

Ingredients	6 portions	Method
Dried black beans	1 cup	Soak in cold water overnight; drain.
Water	1 qt.	Add to beans. Simmer for 3 to 4 hours or until beans are soft, adding more water as needed. Remove bone; discard. Rub soup through fine sieve or blend in blender.
Onion, small, chopped	½	
Celery salt	⅛ tsp.	
Ham bone	1	
Lemon juice	1 tsp.	Add; stir to blend.
Salt	1 tsp.	
Dry mustard	½ tsp.	
Pepper	¼ tsp.	
Red pepper	to taste	
Egg, hard-cooked, sliced thin	1	Put a slice of lemon and egg in each bowl. Pour hot soup over it. Serve.
Lemon, sliced	½	

Cream of Princess Carolyn Soup

Ingredients	8 portions	Method
Carrots, pared, minced	1 cup	Sauté until vegetables are just tender.
Onion, pared, minced	1 cup	
Butter	4 oz.	
Cornstarch	2 Tbsp.	Add slowly; mix well.
Flour	2 Tbsp.	
Chicken consommé	1 qt.	Add; stir well. Cook for 10 to 12 minutes.
Milk, hot	2 cups	Add slowly, stirring constantly.
Parmesan cheese, freshly grated	⅓ cup	Add just before serving.
Salt	½ tsp.	
Nutmeg	⅛ tsp.	
White pepper	dash	
Parsley, freshly chopped	1 Tbsp.	Garnish; serve very hot.

Pam-Pam Steak Soup A La San Francisco

(J. Rivas)

Ingredients	12 portions	Method
Round steak, finely chopped	2 lb.	Braise in heavy pan on top of stove.
Tomatoes, solid pack, minced	1 No. 2½ can	Add.
Onion, pared, minced	1 cup	
Carrots, pared, minced	1 cup	
Celery, minced	1 cup	
Garlic cloves, pared, crushed	4	Add. Cook over low heat for about 1½ hours or until meat is tender.
Salt	to taste	
Pepper	to taste	
Flour	1 cup	Mix together to make roux. Add; simmer for 30 minutes.
Butter	8 oz.	
Beef stock or consommé	3 qt.	Add.
Worcestershire sauce	2 Tbsp.	Add.
Light cream	1½ cups	Add. Serve; garnish with diced croutons.

Avocado Soup

(G. Di Salvo)

Ingredients	12 portions	Method
Butter or margarine	¼ cup	Sauté until soft but not brown.
Medium onions, pared, chopped	2	
Chicken stock	2 qt.	Add; barely simmer, covered, for 15 minutes. Strain. Place onion and garlic in blender or food processor.
Large garlic cloves, pared	10	
Medium avocados, ripe, ½-in. dice	2	Add to blender; add enough of the hot stock to cover. Process until smooth. Add to remaining hot stock. Heat to boiling; remove from heat. Serve hot. Garnish with watercress leaves, minced green onion tops or chopped chives.

Cream of Leek Chantilly

(G. Preuss)

Ingredients	6 portions	Method
Medium leeks, white part only, washed, minced	3 or 4	Gently heat leeks and garlic in butter until translucent.
Garlic cloves, pared, minced	1 Tbsp.	
Butter	¼ cup	
Flour	5 Tbsp.	Add; cook, stirring constantly, for 10 minutes (do not brown).
Chicken stock	1 qt.	Add, a third at a time, mixing thoroughly after each addition.
Chicken bouillon cubes	2	Add; simmer gently for 25 to 30 minutes.
Bay leaves	2	
Heavy cream	½ cup	Add; simmer for 10 minutes. To serve, ladle boiling soup into hot cups or bowls.
Salt	to taste	
White pepper	to taste	
Heavy cream, whipped	1 cup	Garnish each serving with freshly whipped cream.

Pumpkin Soup **(K. Muller)**

Ingredients	*6 portions*	*Method*
Butter Onion, pared, minced	2 oz. 1 oz.	Heat butter in saucepan until melted. Add onion; sauté.
Flour	2 oz.	Add.
Pumpkin, pared, seeded, diced Chicken stock White pepper, ground Bay leaf	2½ lb. 1½ qt. ¼ tsp. 1	Add; simmer until pumpkin is very soft. Strain all of the pulp through a food mill or china cap.
Light cream or milk Butter Nutmeg Cinnamon Ginger Salt	2 cups 2 oz. ¼ tsp. ¼ tsp. ¼ tsp. to taste	Add; heat to a low boil. Taste and adjust seasonings. Serve with croutons.

New England Pepper Pot **(J. Greenwalt)**

Ingredients	*6-8 portions*	*Method*
Large russet potatoes, pared, diced Medium onions, pared, diced Celery ribs, diced Medium bell pepper, diced	2 2 2 1	Combine in saucepan with water to cover. Cook, covered, until vegetables are tender.
Light cream Hot peppers, crushed Red pepper, diced, optional Parsley Beef base or bouillon Worcestershire sauce	1 qt. ¼ cup ¼ cup ¼ cup 1½ oz. 1 Tbsp.	Add; heat to boiling.
Flour Butter	4 Tbsp. 2 Tbsp.	Add to thicken.

Chicken Lemon Soup **(C. Richter)**

Ingredients	*12 portions*	*Method*
Chicken stock Celery, diced Onion, pared, diced Carrots, pared, diced Converted rice Lemon, sliced White pepper	3 qt. 1 cup 1 ¾ cup ¾ cup 1 ¼ tsp.	Combine; cook for about 45 minutes or until rice is tender.
Lemon juice Parsley, chopped Basil Oregano	1 Tbsp. 1 Tbsp. 1 tsp. ½ tsp.	Add; remove from heat.
Sour cream or yogurt Egg yolks	1 cup 2	Combine; beat well. Add several cups of the hot soup; combine thoroughly. Pour back into soup; combine thoroughly. Taste and adjust seasonings.
Chicken meat, diced	1 cup	Add; serve immediately.

Mock Turtle Soup
(H. Frank)

Ingredients	8 portions	Method
Carrot, pared, chopped	1	Sauté.
Celery rib, chopped	1	
Onion, pared, chopped	1	
Garlic clove, pared, chopped	1	
Butter	1 oz.	
Flour	1 oz.	Add; combine thoroughly.
Water	½ gal.	Add slowly; heat to boiling.
Beef gravy base	2 oz.	Dissolve in little warm water in small bowl; add.
Chicken base	1 oz.	
Water, warm	as needed	
Allspice	½ tsp.	Add; cook slowly for 1 hour. Strain through cheese-cloth.
Thyme	½ tsp.	
Coriander	½ tsp.	
Bay leaf	1	
Clove	1	
Nutmeg	¼ tsp.	Add.
Ketchup	½ cup	
Tomato purée	1 No. 2 can	Add; heat through.
Lemon rind	1	
Worcestershire sauce	to taste	
Sugar	to taste	
Sherry	2 cups	Add just before serving.
Eggs, hard-cooked, diced	2	

Southern Bean Soup
(W. O'Neill)

Ingredients	6 portions	Method
Dried Northern beans	2 cups	Wash beans. Heat water to boiling; add beans. Boil for only 2 minutes. Cover; remove from heat; let stand for 1 hour (equal to 12 to 15 hours soaking in cold water).
Water	12 cups	
Ham bone, meaty	1	Add to beans in soaking water. Heat to boiling; reduce heat. Simmer, tightly covered, for about 2 hours or until beans are almost tender.
Onion, pared, minced	1	
Garlic cloves, pared, crushed	2	
Small bay leaf	1	
Potatoes, pared, cooked, mashed	1 cup	Add; heat to boiling.
Celery, thinly sliced	1 cup	
Carrots, pared, raw, diced	1 cup	
Salt	to taste	Taste and adjust seasonings; simmer for 1 hour. Remove ham bone; cut off meat. Dice meat; return meat to soup. Heat to boiling, stirring carefully to avoid breaking beans.
Pepper	to taste	
Heavy cream or evaporated milk	½ cup	Add; stir into soup just before serving.

Hungarian Goulash Soup (S. Nicas)

Ingredients	10 portions	Method
Bacon, minced	4 oz.	Render bacon; add onions. Sauté until light brown.
Onions, pared, diced	1 lb.	
Beef shank, ½-in. dice	2 lb.	Add.
Bouquet garni (1 Tbsp. caraway seeds, 2 bay leaves, 1 tsp. marjoram and crushed white peppercorns to taste)	1	
Flour	2 Tbsp.	Sprinkle over meat; stir.
Tomato paste	3 Tbsp.	Add; stir well.
Hungarian paprika	3 Tbsp.	
Garlic cloves, pared, minced	4	
Beef stock, boiling	1 gal.	Add; simmer for 1 hour or until meat is tender.
Potatoes, pared, ¼-in. dice	2 lb.	Add; simmer for 30 minutes. Remove and discard bouquet garni. Taste and adjust seasonings. Serve as an appetizer in a small earthenware dish; garnish with fines herbes.

Cold Mussel Soup (E. Mauti)

Ingredients	10 portions	Method
Mussels, scrubbed, beards removed	100	Place mussels in freezer 10 minutes before steaming so they will open faster. Heat large pan, covered, over high heat for about 5 minutes. Add mussels; heat mussels, covered, shaking pan occasionally to heat mussels evenly. When mussels open, let them steam for 1 to 2 minutes; remove from pan; reserve all juices. Remove mussels from shells; reserve 10 of the best half shells and 10 of the plumpest mussels. Discard remaining shells.
Dry white wine	½ cup	Heat in small pan to boiling.
Water	½ cup	
Leeks, white part only, cleaned, julienne	1 cup	Poach separately in boiling wine mixture for about 30 seconds. Separately reserve leeks, carrots and cooking liquid.
Carrots, pared, julienne	1 cup	
Leek, green part only, cleaned, chopped	½ cup	Combine with reserved mussel liquid, remaining mussels and reserved vegetable poaching liquid in saucepan. Heat to boiling; simmer until reduced by half.
Celery, chopped	½ cup	
Shallots, chopped	2	
White peppercorns, crushed	4	
Thyme	to taste	
Bay leaf, crushed	½	
Butter, unsalted, room temperature	2 Tbsp.	Mix; add to soup; cook, stirring constantly, over low heat for 15 minutes. Pass through food mill; let cool (this should make 2 cups of soup base).
Flour	1 Tbsp.	
Heavy cream	2 cups	Add to soup base (add more cream to make 1 quart, if necessary). Strain; refrigerate until well chilled. To serve, pour soup into bowls; in the center of each serving, float a reserved mussel on a reserved half shell with some of the reserved vegetable julienne.

Gulf Coast Bouillabaisse

(M. Collins)

Ingredients	6 portions	Method
Assorted fish (a selection of at least 4 of mullet, grouper, catfish, cod, haddock or red snapper), cut into 2-in. squares	2 lb.	Place fish heads and bones, onion, celery and carrots in small stockpot. Reserve fish. Add enough water to cover. Boil for 2 hours; reserve.
Onions, medium dice	2 oz.	
Celery, medium dice	2 oz.	
Carrots, medium dice	2 oz.	
Butter, clarified	¼ cup	Sauté in another small stockpot until lobster shell turns red. Remove lobster; reserve.
African rock lobster tails, cut into ½-in. pieces	2	
Medium yellow onions, pared, diced	2	
Leeks, white part only, washed, sliced	3	
Garlic cloves, pared, crushed	5	
Saffron	½ tsp.	
Medium bay leaves	2	
White wine	1 cup	Add; cook, covered, for 15 minutes. Add reserved fish; cook, covered, for 15 minutes. Add reserved lobster pieces; heat to boiling. Taste and adjust seasonings; remove from heat. Serve on garlic toast.
Chicken stock	1 cup	
Reserved fish stock	1 cup	
Tomatoes, fresh or canned, chopped	1 lb., 8 oz.	
Fennel, dry or fresh	½ tsp.	
Clams, brushed clean, or mussels, scrubbed, beards removed	15	

Goulash Soup

(J. Eidmann)

Ingredients	6 portions	Method
Medium onions, pared, thinly sliced	2	Sauté over medium heat until onions are golden.
Oil	1 Tbsp.	
Stew meat (beef), ¼-in. dice	1 lb.	Add; sauté for 5 minutes.
Flour	2 Tbsp.	Add; stir well.
Paprika	1 Tbsp.	
Tomato paste	1 Tbsp.	
Water	1 qt., 3 cups	Add; heat, stirring constantly, to boiling.
Beef base	2 tsp.	Add; simmer over low heat for about 1 hour.
Salt	¼ tsp.	
Black pepper, ground	⅛ tsp.	
Thyme	pinch	
Medium potatoes, pared, diced	2	Add; simmer until potatoes are cooked.
Lemon rind	¼ tsp.	Combine; dice; add.
Caraway seeds	⅛ tsp.	
Garlic clove, pared	1	
Sour cream	1 Tbsp.	Add (do not boil). Serve with crisp French or sourdough bread.

Cream of Artichoke Soup (M. Gustin)

Ingredients	12 portions	Method
Artichoke bottoms	12	Remove outer leaves; discard. Cut artichokes into eighths.
Water Lemon juice	2 qt. ¼ tsp.	Mix; add artichokes; let sit for about 5 minutes to prevent discoloration.
Water	1 qt., 2 cups	Heat to boiling; add artichokes; simmer until tender.
Butter Onions, pared, minced	6 oz. 2	Meanwhile, heat butter in 3-qt. saucepan until melted. Add onions; sweat. Remove from heat.
Flour	¼ cup, 1 Tbsp.	Add; combine thoroughly. Cook, stirring, for 1 minute. Remove from heat. Strain stock through sieve into roux. Reserve artichokes in sieve. Beat stock until thick; simmer for 10 minutes. Add reserved artichokes.
Egg yolks Heavy cream	4 1 cup	Mix; beat. Ladle 2 cups of the soup into the mixture; mix well; pour mixture back into soup.
Lemon juice White pepper Nutmeg	1 tsp. pinch pinch	Add; taste and adjust seasonings. Remove from heat. Ladle soup into heated cups or terrine. Garnish with chives; serve.

Avocado and Cucumber Soup (R. Marshall)

Ingredients	4 portions	Method
Onion, pared, chopped Medium mushrooms, sliced Butter	1 6 as needed	Sauté slowly until glazed but not brown.
Small garlic clove, pared, crushed Salt	1 ½ tsp.	Combine; add; reserve.
Chicken broth, strong	1 qt.	Heat to boiling; add reserved vegetable mixture.
Cucumbers, pared Avocado, pared	2 ½	Place in blender or food processor. Process until smooth; add to chicken broth; simmer for 5 minutes.
Cucumber, pared, parboiled, drained Avocado, pared, diced	½ 1	Combine; add to simmering chicken broth, stirring lightly.
Light cream	1 cup	Add; taste and adjust seasonings; serve immediately.

SALADS

A salad can start a meal and cleanse the palate, or become the meal itself: (clockwise from top) Curried Banana Salad, Salad Colorado and Calamari Salad.

Salads have become very popular in recent times, probably because of a more health-conscious public that is looking for nutritious food alternatives. Most food establishments now offer a wide variety of salads on the menu.

Salads can be served as an appetizer, as a side dish, as a main dish or as a dessert. Most common salads used today are made with fruit, greens, vegetables or gelatin.

Appetizer salads served as a first course often substitute for more elaborate first courses. They should stimulate the appetite, and have fresh, crisp ingredients. Preportioned salads should be large enough to be served as a separate course, but not too large to be filling. Flavorful ingredients should be used to add appeal. An attractive arrangement also is important because visual appeal stimulates the appetite.

Accompaniment salads are served with the main course. They must balance with the rest of the meal and be light and flavorful, but not too rich. Heavier salads such as potato or macaroni should only be served if the main dish is light.

Main-course salads have become especially popular on lunch menus. They should be large enough to be considered a main dish and contain a good amount of protein. Main course salads should offer enough variety to be balanced in textures and flavors. The portion size gives room for imagination and creativity.

Dessert salads are usually sweet and can contain fruit, nuts, sweetened gelatin and cream. They should be served either as a breakfast item, as dessert or on a party buffet.

Whatever the salad, the ingredients used should be fresh. The basic ingredients include salad greens; raw vegetables; cooked, pickled or canned vegetables; starches; fruits; and protein foods.

Selection and correct handling of fresh ingredients is extremely important. Proper refrigeration, washing and draining of the salad is also a critical step in making a good salad. Learning these simple procedures should ensure a product that is clean, crisp, cool and delicious. —*Dean Jaramillo*

Curried Banana Salad   (L. Haines)

Ingredients	6 portions	Method
Banana (not too ripe), sliced	1	Combine.
Rice, cooked	¾ cup	
Seedless grapes, canned	¼ cup	
Celery, sliced	⅛ cup	
Peanuts, chopped	⅛ cup	
Red pimentos, diced	⅛ cup	
Mayonnaise	½ cup	Mix; add; refrigerate before serving.
Light cream	⅛ cup	
Lemon juice	to taste	
Curry	to taste	
Dry mustard	to taste	

Calamari Salad   (B. Cutino)

Ingredients	10 portions	Method
Squid, peeled, cleaned	4 lb.	Poach tubes and tentacles of squid in strong court bouillon until tender. Let cool; cut tubes into ½-in.-thick rings. Leave tentacles whole.
Court bouillon	as needed	
Red bell pepper, medium dice	8 oz.	Combine with squid rings and tentacles; combine well. Refrigerate for at least 12 hours before serving.
Sweet onion, pared, medium dice	8 oz.	
Tomato, peeled, seeded, medium dice	8 oz.	
Parsley, chopped	1 oz.	
Olive oil	6 oz.	
Lemon juice	4 oz.	
Oregano	1 Tbsp.	
Sweet basil	1 Tbsp.	
Garlic cloves, pared, chopped	1 tsp.	
Salt	1 tsp.	
White pepper	½ tsp.	

Salad Colorado   (S. Krauss)

Ingredients	8 portions	Method
Carrots, pared, cooked, julienne	4 oz.	Toss vegetable with enough of the vinaigrette to moisten. Taste and adjust seasonings. Place leaves on salad plates. Top each with tossed vegetables. Garnish with heart of lettuce.
Yellow squash, seeded, skin on, julienne	4 oz.	
Zucchini, seeded, skin on, julienne	4 oz.	
Bibb or curly leaf lettuce	1 head	
Vinaigrette	as needed	

Brazil Nut-Chicken Salad   (M. Reynolds)

Ingredients	4-6 portions	Method
Chicken meat, cubed	3 cups	Sauté quickly to sear.
Sharp Cheddar cheese, grated	1 cup	Combine.
Celery, diced	1 cup	
Brazil nuts, chopped	½ cup	
Onion, pared, grated	2 Tbsp.	
Lemon juice	1 Tbsp.	
Lemon rind, grated	1 tsp.	
Salt	½ tsp.	
Freshly ground pepper	⅛ tsp.	
Mayonnaise	as needed	Add just enough to moisten thoroughly. Place in greased baking dish; garnish with nuts. Bake at 350F for 25-30 minutes.
Brazil nuts, slivered	as needed	

Verduras y Ensaladas   (C. Wendt)

Ingredients	6 portions	Method
Ground meat	1 lb.	Sauté.
Onions, pared, minced	2	
Lard	2 Tbsp.	
Tomatoes, puréed	10 oz.	Add.
Blanched almonds, sliced	1 Tbsp.	
Pine nuts	1 Tbsp.	
Candied citrons, diced	2	
Vinegar	2 Tbsp.	Add; simmer over low heat until thick.
Sugar	1 tsp.	
Ground cinnamon	½ tsp.	
Long green chiles	1 dozen	Toast; keep wrapped in damp cloth for 30 minutes. Remove skins; slit; remove veins and seeds. Stuff with meat mixture.
Flour	as needed	Coat peppers with flour; dip into egg. Deep fry until golden. Remove; drain; reserve.
Egg, beaten	as needed	
Tomatoes, chopped	1 lb., 8 oz.	Combine; purée; strain.
Onion, pared, chopped	1	
Cinnamon stick	1	
Lard	1 Tbsp.	Sauté puréed mixture in lard.
Stock	1 cup	Add; simmer to reduce. When thick, add reserved chiles; let simmer briefly.
Salt	to taste	
Pepper	to taste	

Vinaigrette Salad Dressing   (J. Jones)

Ingredients	2 qt.	Method
Small green bell pepper, diced	1	Combine.
Small red onion, pared, diced	1	
Tomato, ripe, diced	1	
Pimentos, diced	½ cup	
Pecans, chopped	½ cup	
Parsley, minced	⅓ cup	
Red wine vinegar	3 cups	Combine; pour over. Refrigerate overnight.
Vegetable oil	3 cups	
Sugar	1 cup	
Tomato paste	¾ cup	
Salt	1½ Tbsp.	
Black pepper, coarsely ground	1½ Tbsp.	

Cognac Dressing   (W. Daffinger)

Ingredients	15-20 portions	Method
Mayonnaise	1 cup	Combine thoroughly.
Ketchup	½ cup	
Lemon, juice of	½	
Hot pepper sauce	dash	
Worcestershire sauce	to taste	
Salt	to taste	
Pepper	to taste	
Cognac	2 oz.	Add; add more lemon juice if needed.

Honey Salad Dressing   (P. Montan)

Ingredients	6 portions	Method
Mayonnaise	10 oz.	Combine thoroughly; reserve in refrigerator.
Vegetable oil	½ cup	
Honey	¼ cup	
Small onion, pared, minced	1	
Lemon, juice of	½	
Yellow mustard	½ tsp.	
Parsley, minced	½ tsp.	
Hot pepper sauce	2 dashes	
Salt	pinch	
Mixed salad greens (romaine, escarole, chicory and watercress)	6 cups	Tear into bite-size pieces; place in large wooden salad bowl.
Medium mushrooms, thinly sliced	6	Add.
Medium tomatoes, cut into wedges	2	
Chives, minced	2 Tbsp.	
Eggs, hard-cooked, diced	2	Sprinkle over salad.
Small shrimp, 51-60	1 cup	Sprinkle over salad. Drizzle reserved dressing over salad; let stand for 10 minutes; serve on chilled plates.

Chicken Salad Bengal
(H. Roth)

Ingredients	4 portions	Method
Cucumber, pared, pulp removed, diced	½ cup	Sprinkle salt over cucumber; combine thoroughly; let stand for 30 minutes. Drain; reserve.
Salt	¼ tsp.	
Chicken, cooked, skinned, ½-in. dice	2 cups	Combine; reserve.
Long-grain rice, cooked	1 cup	
Apple or pear, with skin, diced	1 cup	
Dark seedless raisins	⅓ cup	
Coconut, shredded	⅓ cup	
Almond slivers, toasted	¼ cup	
Peanut or vegetable oil	1 Tbsp.	Heat oil in small saucepan; add curry powder; cook over low heat for several seconds (do not let curry burn); let cool.
Curry powder	2 Tbsp.	
Mayonnaise	½ cup	Mix; add to curry mixture. Combine reserved chicken mixture and reserved cucumber; add dressing. Combine thoroughly. Refrigerate for 1 hour.
Yogurt, plain, lowfat	½ cup	
Lemon juice	1½ tsp.	
Salt	¼ tsp.	
Butter-leaf lettuce	as needed	Line platter or serving plates with lettuce leaves; mound salad in center; sprinkle with scallions.
Scallions, finely sliced	¼ cup	

Zucchini Salada - Low Calorie
(M. Collins)

Ingredients	6 portions	Method
Zucchini, unpared	4	Wash zucchini; thinly slice. Reserve in ice water.
Sour cream	3 Tbsp.	Mix well.
Wine vinegar	3 Tbsp.	
Lowfat yogurt	3 oz.	
Jalapeño pepper, chopped	2 Tbsp.	Fold in. Drain ice water; pat dry reserved zucchini. Pour dressing over zucchini. Refrigerate for 3 hours or overnight.
Salt	to taste	

German Beef and Potato Salad
(A. Davis)

Ingredients	12-16 portions	Method
Potatoes	4 lb.	Boil in skins until tender; pare; slice; reserve.
Beef bouillon cubes	4	Dissolve bouillon in water; reserve.
Water, hot	1 cup	
Bacon slices, diced	12	Sauté until crisp; remove; reserve.
Onions, pared, diced	2 cups	Sauté in drippings until tender but not brown.
Beef, cooked, diced	1 qt.	Combine with onion mixture, reserved potatoes, reserved beef broth and reserved bacon; toss thoroughly; refrigerate. To serve, line platter or bowl with Boston or romaine lettuce; spoon salad onto leaves; garnish with tomato wedges and hard-cooked eggs.
Red-wine vinegar with garlic	1 cup	
Vegetable oil	1 cup	
Dill pickles, diced	2	
Prepared mustard	4 Tbsp.	
Horseradish	2 Tbsp.	
Salt	to taste	

Blue Cheese Dressing (J. Marzina)

Ingredients	2 qt.	Method
Mayonnaise	1 qt.	Combine.
Vinegar	½ cup	
Parsley, chopped	2 Tbsp.	
Salt	1 Tbsp.	
Worcestershire sauce	dash	
Blue cheese	1 lb.	Crumble; fold in.

Polynesian Spinach Salad (R. Werth)

Ingredients	6 portions	Method
Spinach, fresh	½ lb.	Rinse with cold water; dry thoroughly. Remove stems; tear into bite-size pieces; refrigerate until serving time.
Soy sauce	1 oz.	Combine thoroughly.
Sesame oil	1 oz.	
Cider vinegar	1 oz.	
Sugar	1 tsp.	
Garlic clove, pared, crushed	½	
Sesame seeds, toasted	1¼ Tbsp.	Just before serving, toss spinach and dressing in large bowl; sprinkle sesame seeds over salad.

Molded Green Bean Salad (E. Gass)

Ingredients	6 portions	Method
Green beans, finest cut	1 15½-oz. can	Drain beans; reserve liquid; add enough water to liquid to make 3 cups; reserve liquid and beans separately.
Unflavored gelatin	1 Tbsp.	Dissolve gelatin in water; reserve.
Water, cold	¼ cup	
Lemon-flavored gelatin	3 oz.	Heat reserved bean liquid to boiling; add reserved unflavored gelatin and lemon-flavored gelatin; heat, stirring, until dissolved. Add vinegar. Refrigerate until slightly thick.
Vinegar	2 Tbsp.	
Onion, pared, minced	½ cup	Stir in with reserved beans; pour into 1½-qt. pan or 12 4-oz. molds. Refrigerate until firm; unmold.
Celery, chopped	½ cup	
Water chestnuts, diced	½ cup	
Tangy Sauce	recipe follows	Serve on crisp greens with Tangy Sauce.

Tangy Sauce (E. Gass)

Ingredients	6 portions	Method
Mayonnaise	1 cup	Combine thoroughly; serve with Molded Green Bean Salad.
Cucumber, pared, grated, drained	½ cup	
Green bell pepper, minced	½ cup	
Vinegar	2 tsp.	
Salt	½ tsp.	
Pepper	pinch	

Duquesne Chef Salad   (J. Lubinski)

Ingredients	6 portions	Method
Bibb lettuce	3 heads	Wash; dry thoroughly; reserve in refrigerator until crisp.
Peanut oil	1½ cups	Combine thoroughly.
Raspberry vinegar	½ cup	
Onion, pared, minced	1 Tbsp.	
Shallot, minced	1	
Dijon-style mustard	1 tsp.	
Lemon, juice of	½	
Garlic clove, pared, crushed	½	
Parsley, chopped	pinch	
Worcestershire sauce	to taste	
Salt	to taste	
Pepper	to taste	
Eggs, hard-cooked, chopped	3	Cut reserved lettuce in half; arrange each half on serving plate. Pour about 2 oz. of the dressing over each; sprinkle with eggs and parsley.
Parsley, chopped	as needed	

Caper Dressing   (B. Bardy)

Ingredients	3 cups	Method
Salt	½ tsp.	Mash in mortar with pestle to form a paste.
Cumin, ground	½ tsp.	
Dillweed, chopped	½ tsp.	
Garlic clove, pared, crushed	¼ tsp.	
Olive oil	1¾ cups	Add; combine thoroughly. Store in sealed container in refrigerator (best when made a day ahead).
Capers, washed, dried, minced	1 3-oz. jar	
Lemon juice	⅓ cup	
Black pepper, freshly ground	½ tsp.	
Pimentos, ¼-in. dice	¼ cup	

Zucchini Salad   (R. Werth)

Ingredients	10 portions	Method
Zucchini, pared	1½ lb.	Cut lengthwise into 2-in. pieces. Parboil in salted water for about 2 minutes until al dente; drain; refrigerate.
Garlic, pared, crushed	1 tsp.	Rub bowl with garlic.
Onions, pared, julienne	¾ lb.	Add with chilled zucchini; toss lightly; reserve.
Green bell peppers, julienne	3	
Celery, julienne	6 oz.	
Sugar	6 oz.	Mix.
Salt	¼ Tbsp.	
Cider vinegar	1 cup	Add small amount of the vinegar.
Vegetable oil	1 pt.	Gradually add.
Sesame seeds, toasted	1¼ Tbsp.	Add with remaining vinegar. Add to reserved salad; toss.
Fennel seeds	¼ Tbsp.	
Cherry tomatoes	¼ pt.	Garnish.

Monterey Bay Prawns Tail Salad

(M. Vedrines)

Ingredients	6 portions	Method
Prawns, 6-10	24	Cook prawns in court bouillon; remove shells.
Court bouillon	as needed	
Egg yolks	4	Mix; add prawns; marinate for 30 minutes. Remove prawns; reserve.
Tomato sauce, thick	2 oz.	
Brandy	½ oz.	
Worcestershire sauce	to taste	
Paprika	1 Tbsp.	
Cayenne pepper	to taste	
Olive oil	4 oz.	Add; heat.
Crème fraîche	2 oz.	Add; add reserved prawns.
Salt	to taste	
Pepper	to taste	
Truffle, thin julienne	1	Sprinkle over prawns.
Chervil	to taste	
Tarragon	to taste	
Salinas butter lettuce	6 hearts	Add just before serving.

Marinated Beef Salad

(K. Muller)

Ingredients	4-6 portions	Method
Beef, cooked, diced	1 lb.	Combine.
Green bell peppers, ½-in. dice	2	
Tomatoes, peeled, seeded	3	
Olives, ripe, pitted	1 cup	
Red onion, pared, sliced	4 oz.	
Parsley, chopped	1 Tbsp.	
Medium mushrooms, cut into quarters	3 oz.	Add; reserve.
Salt	¾ tsp.	Mince together.
Garlic clove, pared, crushed	½	
Olive oil	½ cup	Add; combine thoroughly. Pour over reserved beef mixture; toss thoroughly. Marinate in refrigerator, tossing occasionally, for 2 to 4 hours. Garnish with wedges of hard-cooked eggs and tomatoes, julienne of radishes and carrot curls.
Red wine vinegar	½ cup	
Black peppercorns, crushed	½ tsp.	
Sugar	½ tsp.	

Lillian Haines Velvet Avocado Dressing

(L. Haines)

Ingredients	1½ cups	Method
Large avocado, ripe, pared, cut into chunks	1	Place in blender or food processor.
Water	¼ to ½ cup	Add; process at high speed for about 1 minute until smooth.
Herbed wine vinegar	¼ cup	
Olive oil	⅛ cup	
Vegetable oil	⅛ cup	
Seasoning salt	1½ tsp.	
Cilantro sprigs, minced	2	
Black pepper, coarsely ground	¼ tsp.	

Caesar Salad A La Meadows (H. Meadows)

Ingredients	6 portions	Method
Garlic clove, pared	1	Thoroughly rub bowl with garlic; discard any remaining garlic.
Anchovy fillets	6	Add; rub into bowl with spoon until crushed.
Dry mustard	¼ tsp.	Rub into mixture with spoon.
Romaine, torn into bite-size pieces	2 heads	Add; toss well.
Egg, coddled	1	Add; toss to coat leaves.
Oil, small part olive oil / Wine vinegar / Medium lemon	¾ cup / ⅛ cup / 1	Add oil; toss lightly. Add vinegar; squeeze lemon juice over mixture; toss lightly.
Worcestershire sauce / Salt	1 tsp. / 1 tsp.	Add; toss lightly.
Parmesan cheese, grated	½ cup	Add; toss to coat leaves.
Croutons	¾ cup	Add; combine gently.
Black pepper	to taste	Lightly grind over. Serve on ice-cold plates.

Salade Alemande (S. Stober)

Ingredients	6 portions	Method
Romaine or bibb lettuce	2 heads	Rinse with cold water; dry on paper toweling. Tear into bite-size pieces; reserve.
Large potatoes, pared / Bacon, cut into strips	2 / ½ lb.	Boil potatoes until tender. Meanwhile, sauté bacon; drain about ⅔ of the pan drippings; discard.
Vinegar / Oil / Salt / Pepper, freshly ground	¼ cup / ¼ cup / to taste / to taste	Mash potatoes in salad bowl. Add with bacon and pan drippings. Add reserved lettuce; toss. Taste and adjust seasonings; serve immediately.

Beverly Hills Salad Dressing (L. Haines)

Ingredients	1 pt.	Method
Tomato juice	1 cup	Place in jar with tightfitting lid; shake well. Can be kept in refrigerator for about a week.
Lemon juice	3 Tbsp.	
Onion, pared, minced or grated	2 Tbsp.	
Tamari sauce	2 Tbsp.	
Dillweed, fresh, chopped, or 1 tsp. dried	1 Tbsp.	
Basil, fresh, chopped, or 1 tsp. dried	1 Tbsp	
Parsley, minced	1 Tbsp.	
Green bell pepper, minced	1 Tbsp.	
Chives, minced	1 Tbsp.	
Scallions, minced	1 Tbsp.	
Mint, dried	1 tsp.	
Honey	1 tsp.	
Gingerroot, pared, minced	½ tsp.	

Salad Niçoise

Ingredients	6-10 portions	Method
Olive oil	6 Tbsp.	Combine thoroughly; reserve.
Peanut or vegetable oil	6 Tbsp.	
Wine vinegar	2 Tbsp.	
Dijon-style or Düsseldorf mustard	2 tsp.	
Salt	1½ tsp.	
Thyme, fresh, chopped, or ½ tsp. dried	1 tsp.	
Garlic cloves, pared, crushed	1 or 2	
Black pepper, freshly ground	pinch	
Green beans	2 lb.	Break beans into 1½-in. pieces. Cook in saucepan in salted water to cover until crisp-tender. Drain; rinse with cold water; drain in colander; reserve.
Green bell peppers, cored, seeded, white membranes removed	2	Slice into thin rounds; reserve.
Celery ribs	4	Trim; cut crosswise into thin slices; reserve.
Cherry tomatoes	1 pt.	Arrange reserved beans, reserved peppers, reserved celery, tomatoes and potatoes in a symmetrical pattern in a large salad bowl.
Potatoes, red-skinned, cooked, pared, sliced	1 lb.	
Tuna	3 7-oz. cans	Flake tuna; add.
Anchovy fillets	1 2-oz. can	Arrange on top.
Black olives, Greek or Italian	10	
Stuffed olives	10	
Small red or Bermuda onions, pared, thinly sliced, or 1 large	2	Arrange over salad.
Parsley, fresh, minced	⅓ cup	Sprinkle parsley and basil over salad; garnish with eggs. Add reserved dressing.
Basil, fresh, chopped, or 1 tsp. dried	2 Tbsp.	
Eggs, hard-cooked, cut into quarters	6	

Cold Spinach Salad

Ingredients	8 portions	Method
Spinach, fresh, stems trimmed	2 bunches	Rinse several times with cold water; drain.
Eggs	3	Beat eggs and sugar in blender or food processor until fluffy.
Sugar	1½ Tbsp.	
Oil	1 cup	Slowly add.
Vinegar	½ cup	Add.
Dry mustard	½ tsp.	
Garlic clove, pared, crushed	1	
Salt	¼ tsp.	
White pepper	¼ tsp.	
Bacon slices, cut into thin strips, crisp-fried, drained	4	Toss spinach with dressing, bacon and eggs. Serve immediately.
Eggs, hard-cooked, diced	2	

Sap Sago Salad Dressing (H. Frank)

Ingredients	2 qt.	Method
English mustard	1 Tbsp.	Mix to form a paste.
Water or lemon juice	as needed	
Eggs	2	Add eggs and half of the vinegar; beat.
Tarragon vinegar	3 Tbsp.	
Olive oil	1 qt.	Gradually add oil, beating constantly.
Heavy cream	3 Tbsp.	As dressing gets thicker, add with remaining vinegar
Sap sago cheese, grated	3 Tbsp.	(if too thick, add more cream).
French mustard	1 Tbsp.	
Garlic paste	½ tsp.	
Salt	to taste	
Pepper	to taste	
Sugar	to taste	
Worcestershire sauce	to taste	
Hot pepper sauce	to taste	

Wilted Spinach Salad (H. Jordi)

Ingredients	4 portions	Method
Spinach	5 bunches	Rinse spinach; remove stems; pat dry; place in wooden bowl.
Butter	3 oz.	Melt butter in skillet; lightly sauté shallots.
Shallots, chopped	1 oz.	
Bacon slices, cooked, coarsely chopped	8	Add.
Brandy	2 oz.	Add; ignite.
Sugar	3 tsp.	Add.
Dijon-style mustard	2 tsp.	
Olive oil	3 oz.	Stir in well; heat to simmering. Pour over spinach;
Red-wine vinegar	2 oz.	toss well. Serve on hot plates; sprinkled with chopped
Lemon juice	3 tsp.	hard-cooked eggs.
Salt	to taste	
Pepper, freshly ground	to taste	

Breakers Dressing (H. Warren)

Ingredients	¾ gal.	Method
Cider vinegar	2 cups	Combine thoroughly to form a paste.
Anchovies, mashed to a paste	8 oz.	
Lemons, juice of	3	
Basil	2 Tbsp.	
Salt	1 Tbsp.	
White pepper	1 Tbsp.	
Mustard	1 Tbsp.	
Garlic cloves, pared, chopped	6	
Oil	½ gal.	Slowly stir in.
Parmesan cheese, grated	1 lb.	Add just before serving.

NOTES

SEAFOOD

*As seafood popularity grows, chefs have new recipe ideas: (clockwise from top) Savannah
Fish Stew, Moules a la Poulette and Cold Poached Fish with Watercress Sauce.*

The fish world presents an enormous source of food. Most fish are edible and nourishing. The fat fishes are salmon, shad, halibut, whitefish, lake trout, pompano, bluefish, catfish, mackeral and eels. The lean fish are sole, haddock, perch, smelt and cod. The water content of all fish is approximately 75%.

The freshness of fish is noticed by the firmness of its flesh, bright eyes, bright red gills, a brightness of scales and a clean, fresh smell. Fish is subject to speedy decay by bacterial action. It should be cooked as soon as possible. If using frozen fish or fillets, do not refreeze once thawed.

Shellfish fall into three common divisions:

–Crustaceans—animals with hard shells such as lobsters, shrimp, langostinas, crab and crayfish.

–Mollusks—a large group of invertebrates including oysters, clams, mussels, scallops, squid and octopus.

–Amphibians—any animal that lives on land and water, such as snails, frogs and turtles.

—*Hermann Rusch*

Moules a la Poulette (S. Nicas)

Ingredients	4 portions	Method
Mussels, well-cleaned	4 dozen	Combine; steam, covered, in shallow casserole until mussels open. Strain stock through cheesecloth. Reduce by ⅔.
Dry white wine	2 cups	
Chives, chopped	1 Tbsp.	
White pepper, freshly ground	1 tsp.	
Parsley sprig, chopped	1	
Thyme sprig, chopped	½	
Bay leaf	1	
Shallots, minced	to taste	
Heavy cream	1 cup	Mix; add a little of the stock to the mixture; return to stock. Discard half of the shells; arrange mussels on platter; place sauce in center; cover each mussel with sauce.
Egg yolks	4	
Parsley, chopped	as needed	Garnish with parsley and chives. Serve with garlic toast.
Chives, chopped	as needed	
Garlic toast slices	12	

Savannah Fish Stew (W. Brun)

Ingredients	4 portions	Method
Fish stock	2 qt.	Mix.
White wine	1 cup	
Licorice-flavored liqueur	to taste	
Olive oil	as needed	Sauté; add.
Leek, white part only, julienne	1	
Fennel bulb, julienne	1	
Yellow squash, julienne	1	
Onion, pared, minced	1	
Carrot, pared, julienne	1	
Garlic clove, pared, minced	1	
Saffron	½ tsp.	
Thyme	¼ tsp.	
Marjoram	¼ tsp.	
Bay leaf	1	
Clove	1	
Black pepper	to taste	
Oysters, cleaned	18	Add; simmer for 45 minutes.
Seafood (cod, flounder, snapper, salmon and shrimp combined as desired), cleaned, cubed	1 lb.	
Salt	to taste	

Cold Poached Fish with Watercress Sauce
(L. Zara)

Ingredients	4 portions	Method
Celery ribs, chopped	2	Sauté for 7 to 8 minutes.
Carrot, pared, chopped	1	
Onion, pared, chopped	½	
Butter	2 Tbsp.	
Dry white wine	2 cups	Add; heat to boiling.
Water	2 cups	
Vinegar	to taste	
Lemon slices	2	
Bay leaf	1	
Salt	to taste	
Pepper	to taste	
Rockfish, 3½ lb., cleaned	1	Place in liquid; add more wine and water to cover if necessary. Cover pan. Poach fish just below simmering for 20 to 25 minutes or until cooked. Remove fish from stock; let cool; skin upper surface.
Sour cream	1 cup	Purée.
Mayonnaise	1 cup	
Watercress, stems trimmed	1 bunch	
Chives, minced	2 Tbsp.	Add; beat well. Taste and adjust seasonings. Spread over skinned portion of fish.
Lemon juice	2 Tbsp.	
Anchovy paste	1 tsp.	
Hot pepper sauce	to taste	
White pepper	to taste	
Hard-cooked eggs, sliced	as needed	Garnish.
Pimento strips	as needed	
Lemon slices	as needed	
Parsley	as needed	

Charbroiled Salmon with Ginger Glaze
(M. Cihelka)

Ingredients	10 portions	Method
Clam juice	1 cup	Heat in saucepan to boiling; reduce to ½ cup.
Soy sauce, light	⅓ cup	Add; heat to boiling.
Orange marmalade	1¾ Tbsp.	
Sugar	1 Tbsp., 1 tsp.	
Molasses	4 tsp.	
Lemon juice	1 Tbsp., 1 tsp.	
Gingerroot, pared, grated	1 Tbsp.	
Garlic cloves, pared, crushed	1 tsp.	
Anchovy fillet, mashed	½	
Cayenne pepper	¼ tsp.	
Orange rind, grated	¼ tsp.	
Cornstarch	1⅓ tsp.	Mix; add; stir until smooth; remove from heat.
Sherry	2 tsp.	
Butter, at room temperature	½ cup	Add; beat; reserve.
Salmon steaks or fillets, 9-10 oz. each	10	Brush fish lightly with butter; sprinkle with bread crumbs. Broil on preheated grill for 3-5 minutes on one side, depending on thickness. Turn over; brush with reserved ginger glaze. Cook for 3-5 minutes. Serve immediately.
Butter, melted	¼ cup	
Bread crumbs	3 Tbsp.	

King Neptune's Delight   (G. Grimeissen)

Ingredients	1 portion	Method
King crab legs, Bay scallops, California shrimp meat	5 oz.	Sauté seafood mixture.
Butter	1 Tbsp.	
Scallions, thinly sliced	2 Tbsp.	Add.
Dry sherry	1 Tbsp.	
Corn bread loaves, cut into 3-¼-in. rounds	2	Place 2 corn bread rounds in heated casserole. Spoon seafood mixture over top; pour sauce over. Serve with broiled tomato.
Cheddar Cheese Sauce	recipe follows	

Cheddar Cheese Sauce   (G. Grimeissen)

Ingredients	1 portion	Method
Prepared béchamel sauce	1 cup	Combine thoroughly (more cheese can be added if desired). Serve with King Neptune's Delight.
Cheddar cheese, grated	2 Tbsp.	
Sherry	1 Tbsp.	
Prepared mustard	½ tsp.	
Garlic, pared, crushed	¼ tsp.	

Fish Velouté   (G. Grimeissen)

Ingredients	5 portions	Method
Butter	3 oz.	Heat butter until melted; sauté onion and celery.
Onion, pared, chopped	1 Tbsp.	
Celery, chopped	1 Tbsp.	
Flour	2½ oz.	Add.
Fish stock	2½ pt.	Add, stirring until smooth.
Salt	to taste	Sprinkle with salt; add peppercorns, bay leaf and clove. Heat to boiling; simmer slowly for 30 minutes; strain.
White peppercorns	6	
Bay leaf	1	
Clove	1	

Crab Meat Sauté Kristina   (J. Kaufmann)

Ingredients	6 portions	Method
Butter, clarified	3 Tbsp.	Combine; sauté.
Mushrooms, fresh, sliced	6 oz.	
Shallots, minced	3 oz.	
Paprika	1½ tsp.	
Cognac	6 oz.	Add; flambé.
Parsley, minced	3 tsp.	Add; heat.
Thyme, whole	1 tsp.	
Salt	pinch	
Crab meat	1½ lb.	Add; heat.
Hearts of palm, sliced	6 oz.	
Heavy cream	1 cup	Add; heat. Serve with saffron rice; garnish with paprika and minced parsley.
Sour cream	1 cup	

Baked Stuffed Lobster Savannah   **(V. Karoli)**

Ingredients	6 portions	Method
Lobsters, 1½ lb. each	6	Drop lobsters headfirst into rapidly boiling water to cover; cook for 15 minutes. Drain; let cool. Turn each onto its back; with a sharp knife, split lengthwise from under the head to the tail, cutting through shell. Remove dark veins along back and small vein behind head. Remove claws and crack; take out meat; reserve; discard shells. Remove meat from body cavity; reserve meat and shell.
Butter	6 Tbsp.	Heat butter in large saucepan until melted; add flour; mix well.
Flour	6 Tbsp.	
Heavy cream	1 cup	Using a wire whisk, stir in cream; add mustard. Cook until thick and smooth. Remove from heat; reserve warm.
Dry mustard	3 tsp.	
Butter	3 Tbsp.	Heat butter in skillet until melted; add shallots; quickly sauté (do not brown).
Shallots, chopped	¼ cup	
Mushrooms, diced	3 cups	Add; cook until firm but tender.
Green bell pepper, diced	1 cup	
Dry white wine	1 cup	Add with reserved lobster meat; cook until heated through. Add reserved sauce; combine thoroughly.
Pimentos, diced	1 cup	
Salt	½ tsp.	
Cayenne pepper	pinch	
Parmesan cheese, grated	1 cup	Place mixture in reserved lobster shells; sprinkle with cheese; dot with butter. Heat in broiler until brown.
Butter	as needed	

Striped Bass Steak with Caper Sauce   **(A. Davis)**

Ingredients	12 portions	Method
Striped bass	4 lb.	Cut into 12 5-oz. steaks. Place in poaching pan.
Onions, pared, thinly sliced	2 cups	Add; heat to boiling; reduce heat; simmer for 12 to 15 minutes. Remove steaks to heated platter; strain stock; reserve hot.
Celery, thinly sliced	2 cups	
Dry white wine	1 cup	
Water	1 cup	
Salt	2 tsp.	
Bay leaves	2	
Butter	2 oz.	Dot each steak with butter; cover; reserve hot.
Egg yolks	2	Heat slightly in double boiler.
Butter, melted	2 oz.	Add; cook over boiling water, stirring briskly, for 1 minute.
Lemon juice	2 oz.	
Butter, melted	2 oz.	Add; cook, stirring constantly, for about 3 minutes or until mixture begins to thicken.
Reserved fish stock	1½ cups	Gradually add, stirring constantly, until sauce is smooth.
Salt	1 tsp.	
Cayenne pepper	to taste	
Capers, well drained	6 Tbsp.	Add; pour sauce over reserved bass; serve immediately.

Scallops with Artichokes and Lemon   (R. Readel)

Ingredients	4 portions	Method
Medium sea scallops, fresh	24 oz.	Pat dry; sauté in skillet until firm.
Butter	2 oz.	
Dry white wine	½ cup	Add; heat over low heat.
Chicken stock	½ cup	
Lemon, juice of	1	
Cornstarch	1½ Tbsp.	Dissolve cornstarch in water; add to thicken.
Water	2 oz.	
Canned artichokes, drained, cut in half	8 oz.	Add; combine thoroughly.
Pimentos, minced	1 Tbsp.	Add; portion into 4 casseroles. Garnish with lemon slice and parsley sprig. Serve immediately.
Parsley, chopped	1 Tbsp.	

Curried Fillets of Fish   (J. Joaquin)

Ingredients	4 portions	Method
Fillets, fresh or frozen (cod, perch, halibut, hake, salmon, lingcod, red snapper)	2 lb.	Place in greased baking pan; reserve.
Celery, minced	1 cup	Heat in saucepan for 5 minutes.
Onion, pared, minced	1 cup	
Margarine or butter	¼ tsp.	
Flour	3 Tbsp.	Stir in.
Apples, minced	½ cup	Add; combine thoroughly.
Curry powder	1 tsp.	
Salt	1 tsp.	
White pepper	¼ tsp.	
Milk, warm	1 cup	Gradually add, stirring constantly. Pour mixture over reserved fish. Bake at 400F for about 30 minutes or until fish flakes easily with fork. Serve with steamed rice.

Salmon Tartare   (H. Bendixen)

Ingredients	4-5 portions	Method
Onion, pared, chopped	½ cup	Combine thoroughly to form a paste.
Parsley, chopped	¼ cup	
Olive oil	3 tsp.	
Anchovy fillets	1 tsp.	
Mustard	1 tsp.	
Vinegar	1 tsp.	
Lemon, juice of	1	
Capers	1 tsp.	
Hot pepper sauce	5 or 6 dashes	
Salt	to taste	
Pepper	to taste	
Red king salmon, skinned, boned, minced	30 oz.	Add; toss lightly. Serve on chilled plate. Garnish with chopped hard-cooked egg.

Marinade for Raw Shrimp   (A. Hruza)

Ingredients	6 portions	Method
Vegetable oil	2 Tbsp.	Combine thoroughly.
Vinegar	2 Tbsp.	
Water	2 Tbsp.	
Lemon slices	2	
Parsley flakes	1 tsp.	
Bay leaf	1	
Black peppercorns	⅛ tsp.	
Thyme	pinch	
Salt	pinch	
Shrimp, peeled, deveined, diced	½ lb.	Add; marinate, stirring frequently for 3 hours; drain. Marinade can be used again.

Fillet of Walleye Pike Veronique   (G. Grimeissen)

Ingredients	5 portions	Method
Shallots, minced	2	Sprinkle in buttered deep pan.
Pike fillets, 6 oz. each	5	Place fillets over; sprinkle with salt and pepper.
Salt	to taste	
White pepper	to taste	
White wine	¼ pt.	Add; cover with aluminum foil or buttered paper. Poach over low heat for 10 to 12 minutes. Remove fish from pan; place on heated plates; reserve covered.
Fish Veloute	recipe follows	Heat stock over high heat until reduced; add veloute sauce and cream.
Heavy cream	¼ pt.	
Lemon juice	to taste	Taste and adjust seasonings.
Worcestershire sauce	to taste	
Salt	to taste	
White pepper	to taste	
Seedless grapes, fresh, peeled, or canned	5 oz.	Add (if using fresh, cook lightly and drain). Cook for several minutes. Spoon sauce over reserved fish. Serve with fleurons and parsleyed potatoes.

Fillets of Fish, Tropicale   (J. Joaquin)

Ingredients	4 portions	Method
Fillets, fresh or frozen (any kind)	2 lb.	Place in greased shallow baking dish.
Sour cream	¾ cup	Combine; place mixture over fish.
Coconut chips	5 Tbsp.	
Canned crushed pineapple, strained	3 Tbsp.	
Egg yolks	2	
Cornstarch	1 tsp.	
Lemon rind, grated	½ tsp.	
Green onion, chopped	¼ tsp.	
Salt	¼ tsp.	
Paprika	to taste	Sprinkle lightly. Bake at 400F for about 30 minutes or until fish flakes easily with fork. Serve with steamed rice.

Seafarers' Pie
(J. de Beus)

Ingredients	4 portions	Method
Butter	4 Tbsp.	Heat butter in skillet until melted. Add flour; cook
Flour	4 Tbsp.	over low heat (do not brown).
Milk, hot	1 pt.	Add; cook, stirring often, for 15 minutes; strain; reserve.
Lobster meat	8 oz.	Sauté.
Scallops	8 oz.	
Shrimp, U/15	12	
Butter	¼ cup	
Paprika	½ tsp.	
Sherry	¼ cup	Add; cook for 3 minutes.
Salt	1 tsp.	Add with reserved cream sauce.
Cayenne pepper	pinch	
Egg yolks	4	Stir in 4 Tbsp. of the sauce into the egg yolks; combine thoroughly; return to mixture. Cook, stirring, until mixture is bubbly and thick.
Sherry	1 Tbsp., 1 tsp.	Remove from heat; stir in sherry. Spoon into casseroles; portion meat evenly.
Bread crumbs, fresh, grated	¾ cup	Combine; sprinkle over top. Heat at 400F for 7 to 10
Butter, melted	5 Tbsp.	minutes until brown.
Parmesan cheese, grated	1 Tbsp.	
Paprika	¾ tsp.	
Potato chips, crushed	¾ tsp.	

Sturgeon Steak Suison Bay
(A. Cline)

Ingredients	6 portions	Method
Sturgeon (or salmon, halibut, swordfish or shark) steaks, 7 oz. each, ½-in. thick	6	Lightly sprinkle steaks with salt and pepper; reserve.
Salt	to taste	
White pepper	to taste	
Cucumbers, pared, seeded, diced	3	Sauté for 5 minutes.
Medium celery ribs, diced	3	
Tomatoes, peeled, seeded, chopped	3	
Butter, melted	¼ cup	
Dry white wine	1 cup	Add; cook until alcohol is burned off.
Dry vermouth	1 cup	
Dijon-style mustard	1 Tbsp.	Add; combine thoroughly.
Worcestershire sauce	1 Tbsp.	
Heavy cream	1 pt.	Stir in; remove from heat.
Place reserved steaks in baking dish or individual baking dishes. Pour sauce over. Heat at 350F for 20 to 25 minutes.		
Dillweed, minced	1 Tbsp.	Garnish.

Fillet of Sole Galveston

(R. Schaeffer)

Ingredients	6 portions	Method
Shrimp, cooked	2½ oz.	Mince.
King crab meat, cooked	2½ oz.	
Bread crumbs, white, fine, dry	1½ cups	Combine; add; combine thoroughly.
Butter, room temperature	4½ oz.	
Cognac	2½ oz.	
Paprika	1 tsp.	
White pepper	¼ tsp.	
Salt	to taste	
Cayenne pepper	to taste	
Sole fillets, 2½ to 3 oz. each	12	Spread 3 Tbsp. of the shrimp mixture over half of the skin side of each fillet to ¼ to ⅜ of an inch from the edge. Brush uncovered edge with egg white; fold other half over filling; press together.
Egg white	as needed	
Salt	to taste	Sprinkle with.
Pepper	to taste	
Lemon juice	to taste	
Worcestershire sauce	to taste	
Flour	as needed	Dredge in flour; dip in egg; then in bread crumbs.
Eggs, beaten	2	
Bread crumbs	as needed	
Butter, clarified	as needed	Sauté until brown on both sides. Heat on lightly greased pan at 300F for about 15 minutes until done. Remove from oven; place on plate. Garnish with chopped parsley and lemon wedge; serve immediately.

Lobster Edwardo

(E. Newman)

Ingredients	2 portions	Method
Lobster	1½ lb.	Drop lobster headfirst in boiling water to cover; boil for 6 to 8 minutes until bright red. Let cool; cut in half, head to tail. Remove meat, leaving claws. Cut meat into bite-size pieces.
Shrimp, 21/25, shelled, deveined	4 oz.	Combine; add.
Lump crab meat	3 oz.	
Butter	4 Tbsp.	Sauté; combine.
Shallots or onion, pared	1 tsp.	
Flour	3 Tbsp.	Sprinkle flour over top; using spoon, gradually add milk so fish is not broken up. Simmer for 3 to 4 minutes.
Milk, warm	2½ to 3 cups	
Salt	to taste	Taste and adjust seasonings; sprinkle with parsley. Place mixture in lobster shell.
Pepper	to taste	
Parsley, fresh, chopped	to taste	
Cheese, freshly grated	4 oz.	Combine; sprinkle over whole lobster. Bake at 350F for 10 to 12 minutes or until golden.
Cracker crumbs	2 oz.	
Sherry	4 tsp.	Sprinkle 2 tsp. of the sherry over each serving.

California Abalone Steak Amadine (K. Sayre)

Ingredients	4 portions	Method
Abalone, large, white, cut into 5-oz. steaks	1 lb., 4 oz.	Pound steaks on each side until tender.
Eggs	2	Combine eggs and milk. Dip abalone into flour; then into egg mixture; then into rice flour. Remove any excess breading.
Milk	1 cup	
Flour	½ cup	
Rice flour	½ cup	
Butter, clarified	4 oz.	Heat grill or large skillet until medium hot. Add butter and abalone. Heat until golden; turn over; heat for 45 seconds. Remove from heat; keep warm (do not overcook).
Butter, room temperature	1½ oz.	Mix butter and lemon juice; spread over abalone. Sprinkle almonds over. Serve with lemon wedge and tartar sauce, baked potato or rice with fried zucchini sticks.
Small lemon, juice of	1	
Almonds, toasted	as needed	

Ramon's Vista Del Mar (R. Marshall)

Ingredients	1 portion	Method
Chicken breast, uncooked	3 oz.	Sauté over low heat for 3 minutes.
Butter	2 Tbsp.	
Medium shrimp, 41-50	5 or 6	Add; sauté for 4 minutes.
King crab legs, red if possible, cut into ¾-in. pieces	2 oz.	Add; toss until barely heated. Remove to plate.
Medium tomato, diced	½	
Large avocado, pared, ½-in. dice	¼	
Salt	to taste	
White pepper	to taste	
Monterey Jack cheese, shredded	1 oz.	Sprinkle with.
Mexican fried rice	as needed	Place serving of rice on plate; heat in oven until cheese barely melts. Remove from oven. Garnish with avocado slices, tomato slice and pitted olives.

Paella (M. Loritts)

Ingredients	4 portions	Method
Lobster tails, split	3	Combine.
Chicken, cooked, cut up	½	
Ham, chopped, or chorizo, sliced	1 lb.	
Shrimp, 41-50	6	
Tomato sauce	3 cups	Combine; pour over.
Wine	¼ cup	
Garlic cloves, pared, chopped	3	
Saffron rice, cooked	3 cups	Place saffron rice over top.
Clams	6	Add; bake at 375F for 20 minutes.
Pimentos	as needed	

The San Francisco Special Crab Enchilada   (R. Marshall)

Ingredients	6 portions	Method
Corn tortillas	6	Heat until soft.
Vegetable oil or lard	as needed	
Crab meat	1½ cups	Sauté; place ¼ cup of the crab meat in center of each tortilla.
Butter	as needed	
Onion, pared, minced	6 Tbsp.	Sprinkle 1 Tbsp. of the onion and a little of the salsa over each tortilla. Roll up; place in shallow baking pan. Pour remaining salsa over.
Prepared salsa	as needed	
Monterey Jack cheese, shredded	as needed	Sprinkle generously over. Bake at 400F for about 10 minutes or until hot and cheese is melted.
Sour cream	as needed	Serve with dollop of sour cream; garnish with olives, avocado and tomato slices and pieces of crab leg.
Ripe olives, pitted	as needed	
Avocado slices	as needed	
Tomatoes, peeled, sliced	as needed	

Scallops and Imported Seedless Cucumbers   (E. Mauti)

Ingredients	4 portions	Method
Tiny bay scallops, cut in half	½ lb.	Combine; toss; refrigerate for 2 hours.
Lime juice	2 Tbsp.	
English cucumbers, 8 in. long	3	Cut into 24 1-in.-thick slices; using a 1-in. cookie cutter, cut to remove skin and make perfect rounds. Using a melon baller, make a shallow well in the center of each slice. Reserve.
Crème Fraîche	2 to 3 Tbsp.	Combine. Drain scallops; add. Place a little of the scallop mixture in the well of each reserved cucumber round.
Lime juice	1 Tbsp.	
Salt	to taste	
Cloves, ground	pinch	
Cayenne pepper	pinch	

Octopus Stew   (M. Agius)

Ingredients	6 portions	Method
Octopus, cleaned	3 lb.	Cut octopus into 1-in. pieces; pound with kitchen mallet. Cook in salted water to cover for 1½ hours; drain; reserve.
Salted water	as needed	
Small onions, pared, diced	3	Sauté in saucepan until onions are translucent.
Garlic cloves, pared, minced	4	
Olive oil	1 Tbsp.	
Tomato paste	8 oz.	Mix well; add; simmer for 15 minutes.
Water	1 cup	
Red wine	1 cup	
Red-wine vinegar	¼ cup	
Small potatoes, pared	8	Add with reserved octopus; heat to slow boil.
Allspice, ground	1 tsp.	Add; cook until potatoes are done. Serve on pasta or rice.
Sugar	½ tsp.	
Salt	to taste	
White pepper	to taste	

Lynhaven Oyster Pot Pie

(J. de Beus)

Ingredients	4 portions	Method
Oysters Dry white wine	1 qt. ½ cup	Poach; drain; separately reserve oysters and poaching liquid.
Butter Shallots, minced	2 Tbsp. 2 Tbsp.	Sauté until lightly colored.
Flour	2 Tbsp.	Add; cook, stirring, for about 5 minutes.
Light cream	1 cup	Add with 1 cup of the reserved poaching liquid; cook, stirring with wire whisk, until smooth. Add reserved oysters; heat to boiling; cook, stirring, for several minutes; reserve.
Egg yolks Worcestershire sauce Lemon juice Salt Chives Hot pepper sauce	2 2 Tbsp. 1 Tbsp. ¾ Tbsp. 1 tsp. 2 or 3 dashes	Combine; beat well. Add to reserved oyster mixture; combine thoroughly (do not boil). Place in casserole or shallow pan.
Cracker crumbs, ground Butter Paprika	½ cup as needed to taste	Sprinkle crumbs over; dot with butter; sprinkle paprika over. Heat in hot oven or in broiler until brown.

Scallops and Avocados in Puff Pastry

(D. Barnikel)

Ingredients	10 portions	Method
Scallops, small to medium (if in liquid, reserve liquid) Shallot, chopped Butter, sweet	1½ lb. 1 3 oz.	Sauté.
White wine or champagne Vermouth Muscatel or port	3 Tbsp. 1 Tbsp. 1 Tbsp.	Add.
Cayenne pepper Chervil Salt White pepper Lemon juice	to taste to taste to taste to taste to taste	Add; simmer until scallops are slightly underdone; remove; reserve.
Heavy cream	⅓ cup	Add with reserved scallop liquid.
Cornstarch Water, cold	½ oz. as needed	Dissolve cornstarch in water; add to thicken; reserve.
Avocados, ripe, pared, seeded, cut into thin slices Butter Lemon juice	3 1 oz. to taste	Sauté; sprinkle lightly with lemon juice.
Puff pastry Eggwash	1 lb. as needed	Roll out 10 5x5-in. squares. Place avocado slices over half of each square; portion reserved scallops over. Pour a little of the reserved sauce over each. Fold pastry over to close; brush sides and top with eggwash. Bake at 150-175F for 15 to 20 minutes or until done. Serve remaining sauce on the side with lemon wedge or star.

Stuffed Shrimp Baja (K. Sayre)

Ingredients	6 portions	Method
Butter	1½ oz.	Sauté until golden; remove from heat.
Green bell pepper, minced	1 oz.	
Celery, minced	1 oz.	
Green onions, minced	¾ oz.	
Flour	5 Tbsp.	Add; combine thoroughly. Return to heat; cook, over low heat, for 3 minutes.
Worcestershire sauce	2½ tsp.	
Dry mustard	2 tsp.	
Heavy cream	7 oz.	Add; simmer until thick.
Dry sherry	1 oz.	Add; combine thoroughly.
Bread crumbs, dry	1 oz.	
Parmesan cheese, grated	1 oz.	
Salt	to taste	Taste and adjust seasonings. Remove from heat; refrigerate until cool.
Crab meat, chopped medium	3 oz.	Add; combine thoroughly.
Cottage cheese	2½ oz.	
Cheddar cheese, grated	2½ oz.	
Shrimp, U/12, peeled, deveined, tails intact	18	Deep-split shrimp down top side, butterfly fashion. Portion stuffing into 18 shrimp cavities; wrap each shrimp with bacon slice; secure with wooden pick. Deep-fry at 375F for 3 minutes or until bacon is cooked. Serve immediately on bed of wild and long-grain rice topped with herbed butter. Accompany with broiled tomato Parmesan and cocktail sauce.
Bacon slices	18	

Frogs Legs Da Vinci (M. Di Salvo)

Ingredients	8 portions	Method
Flour	1½ cups	Combine.
Salt	1 Tbsp.	
Black pepper, freshly ground	to taste	
Frogs legs	48	Dip frogs legs in milk; then in flour mixture; shake off excess flour.
Milk	1½ cups	
Vegetable oil	½ cup	Heat oil. Sauté frogs legs in hot oil in skillet over medium-hot heat for 5 minutes.
Garlic cloves, pared, crushed	8	Add; sauté until golden. Remove frogs legs to large casserole. Bake at 400F for 15 minutes.
Dry vermouth	½ cup	Add to skillet.
Eggs, hard-cooked, chopped	8	Stir in. Remove frogs legs from oven; pour mixture over frogs legs; serve.
Chicken broth	½ cup	
Pimentos, chopped	4 Tbsp.	
Parsley, minced	3 Tbsp.	
Capers	3 Tbsp.	
Lemons, juice of	2	

Shrimp Harding

Ingredients	4 portions	Method
Peanut oil	3 Tbsp.	Heat oil in skillet; sauté shrimp for 2 to 3 minutes.
Shrimp, 16/20, shelled, deveined, ¼-in. dice	1 lb.	
Celery	1 cup	Add; sauté for 2 minutes.
Water chestnuts, sliced	1 cup	Add; combine thoroughly.
Bamboo shoots, diced	1 cup	
Mushrooms, sliced	1 cup	
Water	1½ cups	Add; heat to simmering.
Soy sauce	3 Tbsp.	
Sugar	1 tsp.	
Salt	½ tsp.	
Cornstarch	2 Tbsp.	Dissolve cornstarch in water; add to thicken.
Water	3 Tbsp.	
Snow pea pods, julienne	1 cup	Add; simmer for 2 to 3 minutes until hot.
Rice, steamed	4 cups	Serve on hot plate with steamed rice; sprinkle almonds over.
Almonds, toasted, crushed	as needed	

Baked Clams Robert

Ingredients	4 portions	Method
Littleneck clams	24	Open clams; leave shells partially attached; reserve.
Butter	¼ cup	Heat in 12-in. skillet over medium heat (do not brown).
Medium onion, pared, minced	½	Add; sauté lightly for about 3 minutes.
Garlic cloves, pared, crushed	2	
Prosciutto, minced	½ lb.	Add; toss for about 2 minutes.
Bay scallops, minced	½ lb.	
Bread crumbs, coarse	½ lb.	Add; remove from heat. Combine thoroughly.
Parsley	to taste	
Salt	to taste	Taste and adjust seasonings.
Pepper	to taste	
Sherry	3 oz.	Stir in. Portion bread crumb mixture over top of each reserved clam; place on baking pan.
Swiss cheese, grated	¼ cup	Sprinkle each clam with cheese. Heat at 400F for 20 minutes. Serve with lemon wedges.
Lemon wedges	4	

Sweet and Sour Fish
(S. Inonog)

Ingredients	2 portions	Method
Red snapper, whole, cleaned, scored	1½ lb.	Rinse thoroughly.
Rice wine	½ cup	Combine thoroughly; spread into cavity and over scored sides. Marinate for 15 minutes.
Gingerroot, pared, minced	½ oz.	
Black pepper	⅛ tsp.	
Cornstarch	1 cup	Dredge fish; pat to remove excess cornstarch.
Peanut oil	3 cups	Heat in skillet over moderate heat until fish is crisp and golden; remove from pan; reserve warm.
Pineapple juice	1 cup	Combine in saucepan; heat to boiling.
Fish stock	½ cup	
Sugar	½ cup	
White vinegar	5 Tbsp.	
Tomato sauce	5 Tbsp.	
Salt	to taste	
Small green bell pepper, julienne	1	Add; simmer for 2 minutes.
Small red bell pepper, julienne	1	
Small celery rib, julienne	1	
Small carrot, pared, julienne	1	
Cornstarch	2 Tbsp.	Dissolve cornstarch in water; add to thicken.
Water, cold	½ cup	
Pineapple chunks	1 cup	Add; simmer for 1 minute; remove from heat. Place reserved fish on platter; pour sauce over. Serve with timbale of boiled rice.

Canadian Lobster
(H. Bueschkens)

Ingredients	4 portions	Method
Butter, clarified	2 oz.	Pour butter into skillet over high heat. Add lobster; heat until light brown. Remove lobster; reserve warm.
Lobster meat, boiled, cut into bite-size pieces		
Shallots, chopped	1 tsp.	Sauté in same pan until golden.
Paprika	1 tsp.	Add with reserved lobster; heat for 1 minute.
Cognac	1 oz.	Sprinkle cognac over lobster (cognac should boil into lobster meat almost immediately). Sprinkle liqueur over lobster; heat until reduced by half.
Anise-flavored liqueur	2 oz.	
Heavy cream	10 oz.	Add 8 oz. of the cream; heat over high heat, shaking pan back and forth, until sauce is thick; remove from heat.
Egg yolks	2	Combine with remaining cream; add.
Salt	to taste	
Cayenne pepper or hot pepper sauce	to taste	
Parsley, chopped	1 tsp.	Add; combine thoroughly. Taste and adjust seasonings. Serve over rice pilaf.

Baked Gefilte Fish (A. Cline)

Ingredients	8 portions	Method
Fish fillets, fresh (whitefish, pike, carp)	2 lb.	Combine; grind several times. Place in mixing bowl.
Medium onions, pared, chopped	2	
Medium carrot, pared, grated	1	Add; combine thoroughly; reserve.
Water, cold	½ cup	
Large eggs, lightly beaten	2	
Vegetable oil	2 Tbsp.	
Sugar	1 Tbsp.	
Salt	1 tsp.	
White pepper	pinch	
Vegetable oil	as needed	Brush over bottom of loaf pan or round ring mold.
Green bell pepper rings	as needed	Arrange in mold.
Red onion rings	as needed	
Vegetable oil	as needed	Spoon reserved fish mixture into mold; brush with oil. Bake in water bath, uncovered, at 350F for 1 hour. Remove from mold; turn out onto platter. Garnish with lemon wedges and parsley.

Shrimp A La Stober (S. Stober)

Ingredients	4-6 portions	Method
Shrimp, shelled, deveined	1 lb.	Sauté for 3 to 5 minutes.
Butter, sweet	¼ cup	
Shallots, minced	2 Tbsp.	Add; cook for 1 to 2 minutes.
Anise-flavored liqueur	¼ cup	Pour over; ignite; cook until flame dies.
Tarragon, dry, crumbled	½ tsp.	Sprinkle over.
Salt	to taste	Taste and adjust seasonings. Serve with Hollandaise sauce.
Pepper	to taste	
Hollandaise sauce, prepared	as needed	

Crab Meat Imperial (J. Marzina)

Ingredients	6-8 portions	Method
White bread slices, trimmed, diced	8	Combine to form a paste.
Light cream	1 cup	
Egg yolks	4	
Medium green bell pepper, diced	1	
Medium pimentos, diced	3	
Worcestershire sauce	1 tsp.	
Salt	1 tsp.	
Dry English mustard	½ tsp.	
Add; combine thoroughly.		
Maryland lump crab meat	2 lb.	Lightly fold in (do not break up crab meat). Portion into shells. Bake at 350F for 25 to 30 minutes or until brown.

Poached Red Snapper Bertrum

(H. Aeschbacher)

Ingredients	5 portions	Method
Shallots, sliced	2 oz.	Sprinkle into flat, buttered pan.
Red snapper fillets, 6 to 8 oz. each	5	Sprinkle fillets with salt and pepper. Place fillets on top of shallots.
Salt	1 tsp.	
Pepper	pinch	
Fish stock	1 qt.	Combine; pour over fish. Heat (do not boil). Cover with buttered parchment paper; poach at 325F until fish flakes easily with fork (large pieces should be basted occasionally with stock). Pour off stock; remove fish; reserve warm. Heat stock until reduced to desired consistency.
White wine	1 cup	
Lemon, juice of	1	
Butter	as needed	Combine; add to thicken.
Flour	as needed	
Egg yolks	as needed	Combine; add a little of the sauce to the yolk mixture; return mixture to sauce.
Heavy cream	as needed	
Pineapple slices, fresh, poached	5	Arrange over reserved fish; pour reserved sauce over.
Peach slices, fresh, poached	5	
Avocado slices	5	
Mussels	4 oz.	

Shrimp Parisienne

(S. Stober)

Ingredients	4-6 portions	Method
Shallots, chopped	1 Tbsp.	Quickly sauté so color does not change.
Butter	1 Tbsp.	
Garlic cloves, pared, crushed	½ tsp.	
Shrimp, cooked, shelled, deveined	1 lb.	Add shrimp; sprinkle with salt and pepper; simmer for 1 to 2 minutes.
Salt	to taste	
Pepper, freshly ground	to taste	
Heavy cream	1½ cups	Add; heat until reduced to about half.
Chives	1 tsp.	Taste and adjust seasonings. Serve in small coquille shells or plates. Sprinkle with chives before serving. Serve with hot French bread.

Oyster A La Chef Marion

(M. Loritts)

Ingredients	2 portions	Method
Oysters, on half shell	12	Fill baking dish with rock salt; place oysters on salt.
Butter	3 Tbsp.	Sauté until brown.
Mushroom caps, minced	4	
Sherry	2 Tbsp.	Add; reduce heat.
Crab meat, lobster, shrimp	¾ cup	Add seafood; stir in sauce. Spoon a little of the mixture over oysters; bake at 400F for about 6 minutes until bubbly.
Medium white sauce	½ cup	

Mod Lobster

(R. Readel)

Ingredients	4 portions	Method
Cold water lobster tails, 5 oz. each	4	Horizontally cut lobster tails, leaving bottom body shell intact. Remove meat; cut into ½-in. chunks.
Lemon juice Bay leaf Salt	as needed 1 pinch	Combine; add. Gently poach until firm; reserve.
Large green bell pepper, cut into ¼-in. pieces Large mushrooms, cut into ¼-in. pieces Butter	1 4 as needed	Sauté until limp.
Dry sherry Shallots, minced Pimentos, diced	2 Tbsp. 1 Tbsp. 1 Tbsp.	Add with reserved lobster.
Cream sauce, rich Dijon-style mustard	2 cups 1 tsp.	Combine; add. Taste and adjust seasonings; let cool. Arrange mixture in open, clean lobster shells; heat in shell.
Mornay Glaze	recipe follows	Top with; serve hot.

Mornay Glaze

(R. Readel)

Ingredients	4 portions	Method
Basic white sauce Swiss cheese, grated Parmesan cheese, grated	1 cup 1 oz. 1 oz.	Combine thoroughly.

California Fish and Vegetable Bake

(L. Haines)

Ingredients	4-6 portions	Method
Medium lettuce, finely shredded	½ head	Spread evenly over bottom of buttered shallow baking dish.
Red snapper fillets or steaks Salt Pepper	2 lb. to taste to taste	Sprinkle fish with salt and pepper; arrange layer of fish on top of lettuce; reserve.
Tomatoes, peeled, diced Small zucchini, thinly sliced Green bell pepper, chopped Onion, pared, minced Parsley, minced Garlic clove, pared, crushed Salt Pepper	2 2 ⅓ cup ¼ cup 2 Tbsp. 1 ½ tsp. ⅛ tsp.	Combine; reserve.
Lemon juice Olive oil or butter, melted	2 Tbsp. 1 Tbsp.	Drizzle over reserved fish.
Avocado, pared, sliced Mushrooms, sliced	1 ½ cup	Spoon reserved vegetable mixture over fish; place avocado and mushrooms over vegetable mixture.
White wine	½ to ¾ cup	Pour over all. Bake, covered, at 350F until fish flakes easily with fork.

Shrimps St. Tropez   (H. Locher)

Ingredients	4 portions	Method
Olive oil	1 cup	Heat oil in large skillet. Dip shrimp in flour; sauté for 2 minutes on both sides; remove from pan; reserve. Reduce heat to low.
Shrimp, 20-24, peeled, deveined	1½-2 lb.	
Flour	as needed	
Green onions, chopped, or ½ cup dry chives	1 cup	Add; simmer for 2 to 3 minutes until light brown.
Onion, pared, diced, or ½ cup shallots	½ cup	
Sweet anise, diced	½ cup	
Large tomatoes, peeled, seeded, diced	4	Add; heat to boiling; add reserved shrimps.
Mushrooms, fresh, sliced	1 cup	
Dry white wine	1 cup	
Garlic clove, pared, freshly pressed	4 drops	
Garlic powder	pinch	
Fresh oregano or dry dill	pinch	
Worcestershire sauce	1 tsp.	Add; simmer over medium heat for 3 to 4 minutes.
Hot pepper sauce	½ tsp.	
Salt	½ tsp.	
Cornstarch	1 Tbsp.	Dissolve cornstarch in water; add to thicken. Cook for 2 minutes.
Water, cold	as needed	
White pepper	to taste	Taste and adjust seasonings. Add liqueur and lemon juice. Serve in a casserole or scallop shells. Serve with steamed white rice and dillweed.
Hot pepper sauce	to taste	
Anise-flavored liqueur	½ cup	
Lemon juice	to taste	

Maryland Crab Cakes   (R. Schaeffer)

Ingredients	6 portions	Method
Mayonnaise	2 Tbsp.	Whisk together in deep bowl until smooth.
Worcestershire sauce	2 tsp.	
Lemon juice, fresh	2 tsp.	
Seafood seasoning	1 tsp.	
Onion powder	1 tsp.	
Dry mustard	½ tsp.	
Cayenne pepper	pinch	
Salt	to taste	
Pepper	to taste	
Bread slices, fresh, white, crusts removed, fine dice	4	Combine; add.
Crackers, finely crumbled	8	
Eggs, beaten	2	
Parsley, chopped	1 Tbsp.	
Crab meat, fresh, frozen or canned, drained, cartilage removed, flaked	22 oz.	Add; toss well but lightly. Shape into 12 firm flat cakes or patties.
Flour	as needed	Dust with flour; deep-fry quickly on both sides until golden. Remove; drain on paper toweling. Serve hot.
Vegetable oil, hot	as needed	

Creamed Finnan Haddie

(H. Bazan)

Ingredients	4 portions	Method
Haddock fillets, smoked, 4 oz. each	4	Place in saucepan or skillet in water to cover.
Lemon, juice of	1	Add; heat to boiling (do not overcook); reserve.
Cream sauce Eggs, hard-cooked, chopped	1 cup 2	Combine.
Parsley, chopped	1 Tbsp.	Place reserved fish in casserole. Pour sauce over; sprinkle with parsley.
Green peas Harvard beets Potato, steamed or boiled	1 cup 1 cup 1 cup	Serve with.

Java Seafood Curry

(R. Kinney)

Ingredients	1 portion	Method
Australian lobster, 20/22, cut into chunks Mexican shrimp, 16/20, peeled, deveined Butter	2 oz. 3 1 oz.	Sauté.
Curry sauce Alaskan king crab, cut into chunks Shallots, chopped	3 oz. 2 oz. ¼ tsp.	Add; simmer for 5 minutes.
Parsley	as needed	Arrange rice ring in center of hot serving plate. Garnish with parsley. Spoon seafood curry into ring. Serve with coconut, minced currants, chutney, Spanish peanuts, applesauce or banana slices dipped in lemon juice.

Baked Scallops Donna

(H. Bueschkens)

Ingredients	6 portions	Method
Butter Large scallop shells	5 oz. 6	Heat a little of the butter until melted; brush inside of each shell with butter. Arrange shells on baking pan.
Scallops Salt Pepper	1¼ to 1½ lb. to taste to taste	Place scallops in bowl; sprinkle with salt and pepper.
Cracker crumbs Bread crumbs, fresh	1½ cups ½ cup	Heat remaining butter in small skillet. When foam subsides, add cracker and bread crumbs. Heat, stirring, for 45 minutes until crisp (do not scorch or burn). Spread half of the crumb mixture over bottom of shells. Arrange scallops on top. Evenly sprinkle remaining crumb mixture over scallops.
Heavy cream	½ cup	Pour cream over scallops; bake at 350F for 30 minutes until cream is bubbly and crumbs are golden. Serve immediately.

Lobster Thermidor (R. Hough)

Ingredients	4 portions	Method
Lobster meat, ½-in. dice	1 lb.	Heat in saucepan, stirring gently with wooden spoon, until lobster is cooked through.
Mushroom stems and pieces	6 oz.	
Sherry	¼ cup	
Onion, pared, minced	½	
Paprika	1 tsp.	
Dry mustard	½ tsp.	
Light cream	½ cup	Add; heat to simmering.
Egg yolks, beaten	6	Add; heat, stirring slowly and constantly, until thick (do not boil).
Heavy cream	1 cup	Add cream; heat, stirring, to simmering. Taste and adjust seasonings. Serve over patty shells or toast points.
Salt	to taste	
Pepper	to taste	

Crab Meat Michel (M. Lartigue)

Ingredients	8 portions	Method
Lump crab meat, fresh	1 lb.	Remove any cartilage or shells.
Shallots, minced	4 oz.	Combine; add.
Parsley, minced	1 tsp.	
Garlic clove, pared, crushed	1	
Dry white wine	2 tsp.	Fold in.
Lemon juice	1 tsp.	
Sour cream	½ cup	Stir in; combine thoroughly. Taste and adjust seasonings.
Salt	to taste	
Black pepper, freshly ground	to taste	
Bread crumbs	1 cup	Divide mixture into 8 balls; roll in bread crumbs.
Artichoke bottoms	8	Place balls on artichoke bottoms; dot with butter. Bake at 350F for 15 minutes until brown.
Butter	2 Tbsp.	
Hollandaise sauce, prepared	as needed	Serve immediately with sauce.

Lobster Rarebit Leon (L. Oppenheimer)

Ingredients	25 portions	Method
Milk	2 qt.	Heat until hot.
Vegetable oil	1¼ cups	Combine; stir into. Cook, stirring constantly, until thick and smooth (do not burn).
Flour	1¼ cups	
Dry mustard	2 tsp.	
Salt	1 tsp.	
Paprika	1 tsp.	
Cheddar cheese, grated	1½ lb.	Stir in.
Lobster meat, cut into ½-in. pieces	1½ lb.	Lightly sauté lobster; add.
Toast slices, trimmed	25	Cut toast into triangles. Serve lobster mixture in casserole with toast points for "scooping."

Rainbow Trout, Old Baldy (F. Waskey)

Ingredients	4 portions	Method
Worcestershire sauce Rainbow trout, cleaned	¼ cup 12 oz. to 1 lb.	Pour Worcestershire sauce in pan large enough to accommodate trout. Place fish in pan. Brush sauce inside of fish; turn fish in sauce until moist all over. Marinate, turning often, for 20 minutes. Remove fish (fish should be moist).
Flour, sifted Salt Black pepper	4 oz. 1 tsp. pinch	Combine; dredge fish, dredging body cavity.
Butter, clarified	3 oz.	Place butter in skillet; heat over medium heat until just below smoking point. Place trout in pan; cook on each side until golden. Bake at 375F, turning halfway through, about 8 minutes for 12-oz. trout or until done. Remove from oven; place on heated platter; reserve warm.
Butter Parsley, chopped Medium lemon	3 oz. 2 Tbsp. ½	Discard liquid in pan. Add butter and parsley. Strain lemon juice into pan. Heat to boiling, shaking vigorously, until foamy but not brown. Pour over reserved fish.
Medium lemon	½	Garnish with; serve immediately.

Rolled Fillet of Sole Americaine (H. Rusch)

Ingredients	6 portions	Method
Sole fillet	1	Pound fillet; cut into pieces; rub through sieve into bowl over ice.
Heavy cream Fish velouté Egg white	½ cup ⅓ cup 1	Add cream and velouté; gradually add egg white, whisking constantly, until fluffy and stiff.
Salt Pepper Cayenne pepper	to taste to taste to taste	Add.
Sole fillets, 6 oz. each Salt Pepper	6 to taste to taste	Place each fillet on waxed paper; sprinkle lightly with salt and pepper. Portion stuffing on each fillet about ⅛-in. high. Roll up fillets.
Butter, melted Shallots, chopped Salt Pepper	½ cup 1 Tbsp. to taste to taste	Brush bottom of baking dish with butter. Sprinkle with shallots, salt and pepper. Place fillets side by side, brushing butter between them.
Lemon, juice of Salt Pepper White wine	1 to taste to taste 1 cup	Sprinkle with lemon juice, salt and pepper. Pour wine over. Place a sheet of buttered parchment paper over. Heat to boiling. Heat at 325F for 5 minutes. Remove to warm serving platter; reserve hot.
American sauce	1 cup	Heat liquid in pan until reduced to ⅓. Add sauce; simmer for 2 minutes.
Sour cream Cayenne pepper	½ cup to taste	Fold in; taste and adjust seasonings. Serve with reserved fillets.

Calamari Parmigiana   (B. Cutino)

Ingredients	6 portions	Method
Squid, whole, 5 to 6 oz. each	12	Clean; peel fillet; tenderize.
Flour Eggs, beaten Bread crumbs, fine, seasoned	4 oz. 2 8 oz.	Dredge fillets in flour; then in egg; then in bread crumbs. Stack separately on waxed paper; reserve.
Olive oil Garlic cloves, pared, chopped	4 Tbsp. 2	Sauté until brown.
Tomato sauce Salt Pepper	2 8-oz. cans ½ tsp. ½ tsp.	Add; cook over high heat for 15 minutes.
Parsley, fresh, chopped Basil, fresh or dry	2 Tbsp. 1 Tbsp.	Add.
Butter, clarified Monterey Jack cheese slices	1 oz. 6	Quickly sauté reserved fillets, turning once. Arrange in pan with 2 slices overlapping. Place 1 slice of cheese over each; pour 2 oz. of the sauce over each. Bake at 400F for 3 to 5 minutes or until cheese is melted. Serve immediately.

Sautéed Scallops and Mushrooms   (M. Reynolds)

Ingredients	4 portions	Method
Butter Scallops Garlic salt Mushrooms, sliced	6 oz. 1 lb. to taste 8 oz.	Heat butter in skillet until melted. Add scallops; sprinkle with garlic salt. Add mushrooms; cook over high heat for about 2 minutes.
Dry sherry Green onions, chopped	2 oz. 2 oz.	Add; cook for 2 minutes; reduce heat.
Hollandaise sauce, prepared	¼ cup	Add; cook, stirring constantly, for 1 minute. Pour into 4 casseroles.
Parsley, chopped	to taste	Sprinkle over.

Ceviche Acapulco Style   (C. Wendt)

Ingredients	6 portions	Method
Pompano or haddock fillets Lemons, juice of	1 lb. 5	Rinse fish; remove and discard skin; cut into small squares. Place in china or glass dish; pour lemon juice over; let stand, turning fish pieces with wooden spoon occasionally, for 3 hours.
Tomatoes, peeled, diced	½ lb.	Add.
Pickled serrano chilies Vegetable oil Vinegar Oregano Salt Pepper	4 4 Tbsp. 1 Tbsp. ½ tsp. to taste to taste	Add; combine thoroughly.
Avocados, pared, sliced Onion, pared, sliced	2 1	Serve ice cold in sherbet glasses or shells; garnish with avocado and onion.

Prawn Curry (A. Qureshi)

Ingredients	7 portions	Method
Turmeric	½ tsp.	Soak.
Chili powder	½ tsp.	
Garlic cloves, pared, crushed	½ tsp.	
Coriander	½ tsp.	
Cumin	½ tsp.	
Paprika	½ tsp.	
Cayenne pepper	to taste	
Salt	to taste	
Water	1 cup	
Vegetable oil or butter	as needed	Heat oil; sauté onion until light brown. Add seasoning mixture; heat, stirring constantly to prevent burning.
Onion, pared, minced	1 cup	
Medium tomatoes, peeled, seeded, diced	5	Add; heat, stirring, until tomatoes are dissolved.
Prawns, U/15, peeled, deveined	3 lb.	Add; combine thoroughly.
Water	1 cup	Add; heat to boiling; simmer over low heat for 3 minutes. Serve with rice pilaf and vegetable.

Lobster En Cremé (A. Dumancas)

Ingredients	4 portions	Method
Lobster meat	1 lb., 8 oz.	Lightly dust lobster with flour; sauté in hot butter.
Flour	as needed	
Butter, clarified	6 oz.	
Mushrooms, fresh, sliced	8 oz.	Add.
Whiskey	4 oz.	Add; flambé. When flame subsides, remove; reserve warm.
Chicken stock	2 cups	Heat in same skillet until reduced by half.
Heavy cream	1 cup	Add; heat until reduced and thick.
Dry sherry	4 oz.	Add with reserved lobster mixture.
Egg yolks, beaten	3	Add some of the sauce to egg yolks; return to pan. Taste and adjust seasonings. Serve in a casserole or on pineapple boats.
Salt	to taste	
Pepper	to taste	
Hollandaise sauce, prepared	as needed	Top with Hollandaise sauce; heat in broiler until brown. Garnish with pineapple.

POULTRY

Poultry, probably the most versatile meat, is enjoying new popularity with the concern for leaner meals: Turkey a la Maison (top) and Chicken Florentine (bottom).

Poultry refers to domesticated birds used for food. These include chickens, ducks, turkeys, geese, Cornish game hens, guinea hens, capon and squab.

Chicken comes in many forms:

–Broilers—very young chickens weighing 1½ to 2½ pounds.

–Rock Cornish game hens—special breed of young chicken, very tender and delicate. Usually 5 to 6 weeks old, weighing between 12 ounces and 2 pounds.

–Large broilers—used for frying, barbecuing and roasting. This is the most versatile chicken on the American market today, weighing 1½ to 2 pounds.

–Fryers—a young larger chicken weighing 3½ to 5½ pounds. It has tender flesh and flexible cartilage.

–Capon—a large rooster that has been castrated and fattened for roasting. The flesh is very tender and well-flavored. Capon is expensive.

–Fowl or hen—a chicken who has laid eggs for at least two years and is no longer productive. It can be any weight. It has tough flesh and coarse skin, and should be simmered. It is especially good for soup or stock, salad or chicken entrees.

Turkey has four classifications: fryer-roasters, under 16 weeks old and of either sex; young turkey, five to seven months old with tender flesh but firmer cartilage; yearling turkeys, fully matured and still reasonably tender; and mature turkeys, old turkeys with with tough flesh and coarse skin.

Poultry is one of the cheapest meats that can be put on the table. Compared to other meats, it is the lowest in fat and cholesterol. It is the most versatile menu item. It can be fried, breaded, broiled, poached, braised, sautéed, steamed, stuffed, fricasseed and stewed.

—*Jon Greenwalt*

Turkey a la Maison (K. Loos)

Ingredients	6 portions	Method
Onion, diced	10 oz.	Sauté
Butter	8 oz.	
Dark turkey meat, uncooked, 1½-in. dice	2 lb.	Add; sauté.
Cooked ham, julienne	1 lb.	
Mushrooms, sliced	10 oz.	
Broccoli florets, blanched, drained	1 lb.	Add; sauté
Sherry	⅔ cup	
Mornay Sauce	1½ qt.	Add; simmer 5 minutes.
Onion rolls	6	Cut off tops; hollow out rolls. Spoon turkey mixture into roll bottom; cover with tops.

Dietetic Chicken Florentine (G. Di Salvo)

Ingredients	4 portions	Method
Chicken breast, skinned, boned	1 lb.	Place chicken breasts in sauté pan. Sprinkle with
White pepper	⅛ tsp.	pepper.
Chicken broth	¾ cup	Add; bring to boil; reduce heat. Simmer covered for
Dry white wine	6 Tbsp.	25 minutes. Remove chicken with slotted spoon; reserve broth. Cover reserved chicken; keep warm.
Spinach, rinsed, stemmed, dried	1 lb.	Steam 3 minutes; drain. Reserve.
Water	1 Tbsp.	Combine; stir into broth in pan. Cook, stirring, until
Cornstarch	2 tsp.	thick and bubbly. Cook 2 minutes more.
Neufchâtel cheese, diced	3 oz.	Add; stir until melted.
Lemon juice	to taste	Arrange reserved spinach on plate; sprinkle with
Paprika	to taste	lemon juice. Top with reserved chicken, then sauce.
Lemon, slices or wedges	as needed	Sprinkle with paprika. Garnish with lemon.

Turkey Steak Guacamole (G. Grimeissen)

Ingredients	6 portions	Method
Turkey breasts, boned, skinned	6	Separate supreme from breast meat. Slice breast meat and breast supreme into 4-oz. portions. Pound carefully; do not tear meat. Season and dredge in flour. Reserve.
Flour	as needed	
White pepper	as needed	
Salt	as needed	
Avocado, medium, pared	1½	Dice avocado; sprinkle with lemon juice.
Lemon juice	1 tsp.	
Tomatoes, peeled, diced	to taste	Add to diced avocados. Mix carefully. Warm mixture briefly; do not boil. Reserve.
Salt	to taste	
White pepper	to taste	
Garlic powder	to taste	
Brown sauce	¾ cup	Combine in saucepan; simmer about 30 minutes, until sauce is shiny and smooth; reserve.
Ketchup	2 Tbsp.	
Red jalapeño sauce	¾ tsp.	
Chili powder	1½ tsp.	
Olive oil	1½ Tbsp.	Heat in sauté pan; brown reserved turkey steaks. Remove; reserve.
Monterey Jack cheese, thin slices	6	Top each turkey steak with reserved guacamole and one slice of cheese. Place in 375F-400F oven until cheese is melted. Arrange on plate. Spoon sauce on one portion of each steak. Serve with Mexican or saffron rice.

Stuffed Breast of Turkey (C. Imaz)

Ingredients	4 portions	Method
Butter	3 Tbsp.	Melt in sauté pan until hot but not burned.
Turkey breast, boned, skinned, cut into 1½-in. medallions	8	Flatten medallions between waxed paper with mallet. Sauté in butter on both sides until golden. Remove; drain. Reserve; keep warm.
Veal, lean, ground	8 oz.	Combine.
Mushrooms, finely ground	1 cup	
Shallot, minced	½ tsp.	
Onion, minced	½ tsp.	
Chervil, minced	½ tsp.	
Parsley, minced	½ tsp.	
Tarragon, minced	½ tsp.	
Bread crumbs, soft, fine	½ cup	Soak; press dry. Add veal-spice mixture. Put through food grinder twice.
Madeira	as needed	
Butter	3 Tbsp.	Melt in sauté pan. Add stuffing mixture, cook, stirring constantly, over low heat for about 4 minutes. Spread stuffing over reserved medallions. Roll up jellyroll fashion; secure with wooden picks.
Eggs, beaten	2	Dip turkey rolls in egg; coat with crumbs then nuts. Sauté until lightly brown. Bake at 350F for 5 minutes.
Bread crumbs, soft, fine	½ cup	
Pistachio nuts, chopped, toasted	½ cup	
Butter	as needed	

Chicken Teriyaki
(E. Stocker)

Ingredients	8 portions	Method
Broiler-fryer chickens, 2¼ lb. each	3	Cut each chicken into 8 pieces.
Water	1 qt., 2 cups	Combine; pour about ¾ of the marinade over chicken; marinate in refrigerator for 24 hours. Place marinated chicken in baking pan; heat at 375F for about 25 minutes or until done. Heat remaining marinade to boiling.
Soy sauce	2 cups	
White wine	1 cup	
Brown sugar	6 oz.	
Garlic clove, pared, chopped	¼ tsp.	
Gingerroot, pared, chopped	1 oz.	
Lime, juice of	1	
Cornstarch	as needed	Combine; add to boiling marinade to thicken. Spoon sauce over chicken. Serve with rice pilaf; garnish with fresh pineapple.
White wine	as needed	

Chicken Breast Piccata
(R. Buttner)

Ingredients	6 portions	Method
Chicken breasts, 8 oz. each, boned, skinned	6	Coat chicken with flour.
Flour	½ cup	
Corn oil	½ cup	Heat in skillet; add chicken; sauté until golden.
Butter	2 Tbsp.	
Chicken stock	2 cups	Add; cook until reduced.
White wine	1 cup	
Mushrooms, sliced	2 cups	
Green onions, diced	½ cup	
Lemon, juice of	1	
Salt	to taste	
Pepper	to taste	
Butter	1 Tbsp.	Add. Can be served over a bed of herb rice.

Turkey Thighs French Style
(F. Sonnenschmidt)

Ingredients	4 portions	Method
Turkey thighs, 1 to 1¼ lb. each, boned, lightly pounded	2	Generously sprinkle turkey with salt and pepper. Brush with oil on all sides. Heat in broiler until golden.
Salt	to taste	
Pepper	to taste	
Oil	as needed	
Prepared mustard	2 to 3 Tbsp.	Brush over turkey.
Bread crumbs	½ cup	Combine; cover turkey with bread crumb mixture. Heat at 350F until done.
Butter, melted	2 Tbsp.	
Medium tomatoes, cut in half	2	Combine sugar, thyme, garlic and salt; sprinkle over tomato halves; broil.
Sugar	½ tsp.	
Thyme	½ tsp.	
Garlic clove, pared, crushed	1	
Salt	to taste	
Bacon slices	2	Heat in broiler until crisp. Serve turkey thighs with tomatoes and bacon.

Chicken Cantonese

(E. Jimenez)

Ingredients	4 portions	Method
Broiler-fryer chicken, 3 lb., cut into 8 pieces	1	Marinate chicken in soy sauce and olive oil in refrigerator overnight.
Soy sauce	3 Tbsp.	
Olive oil	2 Tbsp.	
Sesame oil	as needed	Heat in deep skillet to 390F. Remove chicken from marinade; pat dry. Carefully place in hot oil. Heat for about 6 minutes or until golden on both sides; drain. Place in baking pan.
White wine	¼ cup	Add to chicken; cover pan tightly with aluminum foil. Bake at 375F for about 20 minutes or until chicken is tender. Arrange chicken on warm serving platter.
Water	¼ cup	
Soy sauce	2 Tbsp.	
Scallions, chopped	2 Tbsp.	
Chicken stock or water and chicken bouillon cubes	1 qt.	Add to juice in pan; heat to boiling.
Cornstarch	½ Tbsp.	Dissolve cornstarch in water; add to stock. Cook, stirring, until sauce is smooth and thick. Pour over chicken.
Water	as needed	
Cashews, chopped	¼ cup	Sprinkle over chicken.

Chicken and Shrimp Creole

(F. Metz)

Ingredients	2-3 portions	Method
Green bell pepper, julienne	1	Lightly sauté. Remove from skillet with slotted spoon; reserve warm.
Red bell pepper, julienne	1	
Onion, pared, julienne	1	
Vegetable oil	as needed	
Shrimp, 16-20, peeled, deveined	12	Add to pan; sauté. Remove; reserve.
Chicken breasts, 8 oz. each, skinned, boned, cut into ½-in. strips	2	Add to pan; sauté. Return reserved shrimp to pan.
Garlic cloves, pared, crushed	2	Add to pan; sauté.
Chili powder	½ tsp.	
Cumin	¼ tsp.	
Thyme	¼ tsp.	
Allspice	¼ tsp.	
Hot pepper sauce	⅛ tsp.	
Tomato, peeled, julienne	1	Add with reserved sautéed vegetables. Taste and adjust seasonings.
Brown sauce	½ cup	
Chili sauce	2 Tbsp.	
Saffron rice	as needed	Serve chicken and shrimp with okra in ring of saffron rice.
Okra, sautéed	as needed	

Chicken Almond

(J. Blackwell)

Ingredients	4-6 portions	Method
Chicken, 3 lb.	1	Remove bones; reserve. Dice meat; reserve.
Reserved chicken bones Water	 1 qt.	Cook bones in boiling water for 1 hour. Reserve broth.
Vegetable oil Salt Pepper	½ cup to taste to taste	Heat oil; sauté reserved chicken (do not overcook). Remove chicken; sprinkle with seasonings; reserve.
Onion, pared, diced Celery, diced Mushrooms, sliced Water chestnuts, sliced	1 cup 1 cup 1 cup ¾ cup	Add to same skillet; lightly sauté until crisp-tender.
Reserved chicken broth Soy sauce	2 cups 3 oz.	Add; heat to boiling.
Cornstarch Water	2 Tbsp. as needed	Dissolve cornstarch in water; add; cook until thick.
Green peas Rice, steamed Pineapple, fresh, en brochette Almonds, slivered	½ cup as needed as needed 1 cup	Add peas and reserved chicken; serve with steamed rice. Garnish with pineapple and almonds.

Boneless Breast of Chicken and Cognac

(H. Lewis)

Ingredients	6 portions	Method
Teriyaki sauce Cognac Pineapple juice Lemon juice Brown sugar Cornstarch	½ cup ⅓ cup ¼ cup ¼ cup ¼ cup 2 tsp.	Mix for marinade.
Chicken breasts, 7 oz. only, boned	6	Marinate in refrigerator overnight. Remove; reserve marinade.
Butter, melted	as needed	Sauté breasts in butter over medium heat. Remove to platter or hotel pan; keep warm.
Cognac	2 oz.	Add to sauté pan; ignite. Add reserved marinade; stir well.
Heavy cream Mushrooms, fresh or canned, whole Small onions, whole, pared	1 cup 18 18	Add; simmer for about 5 minutes.
Noodles or rice, cooked	1 lb., 2 oz.	Serve chicken and sauce hot over noodles or rice. Garnish with chopped parsley or pimentos.

Capon Chipolata   (F. Metz)

Ingredients	8 portions	Method
Chestnuts	2 cups	Make small crosscuts in chestnut skins. Simmer in boiling water for 3 to 4 minutes. Remove chestnuts, several at a time; peel outer and inner skins while still hot. Cut peeled chestnuts in halves or thirds. Reserve.
Butter	2 Tbsp.	Sauté.
Onion, chopped	1	
Garlic cloves, pared, minced	2	
Pork shoulder meat, ground	2 cups	Add; cook until meat turns gray.
Parsley, chopped	2 Tbsp.	Add; mix. Remove from heat; reserve.
Sage	⅛ tsp.	
Thyme	⅛ tsp.	
Marjoram	⅛ tsp.	
Rolls or bread, stale, diced	2 cups	Combine; soak.
Chicken broth	½ cup	
Eggs	2	Add; combine with reserved chestnuts and reserved pork mixture. Spread on tray to cool. Reserve.
Salt	to taste	
Pepper	to taste	
Capon	8 lb.	Remove giblets and neck; reserve. Clean and dry cavity. Season cavity with salt and pepper. Fill with reserved stuffing. Close cavity opening with clamps or string. Tie strips of bacon across entire capon. Roast in pan with reserved neck at 375F for approximately 2 hours 20 minutes, basting occasionally.
Salt	to taste	
Pepper	to taste	
Bacon, sliced	as needed	
Sweet potatoes, pared, turned	3	After capon has roasted for 1 hour, add.
Carrots, pared, turned	3	
Potatoes, pared, turned	8	
Turnips, pared, turned	3	After capon has roasted for 1 hour and 20 minutes, add. When all vegetables are cooked, remove. Reserve; keep warm.
Mushroom caps	8	
Chestnuts, peeled	10	
Brussels sprouts, cooked	1 lb.	Add to reserved vegetable mixture. Reserve warm.
Pork sausages, cooked	8	
Bacon, ¼-in. slices, cooked	8 oz.	
Chicken broth	1 cup	Remove roast from pan; reserve warm. Pour off fat from pan; deglaze drippings with broth, wine and brown sauce. Adjust seasonings. To serve, remove strings and bacon strips from capon. Place stuffing on serving tray and cover with sliced breast meat. Arrange vegetable mixture in place of breast.
White wine	½ cup	
Brown sauce	½ cup	

Breast of Chicken, Jerusalem (T. Rosemond)

Ingredients	4 portions	Method
Chicken breasts, 8 oz. each, skinned, boned	4	Sprinkle seasonings over chicken.
Basil	1 tsp.	
Salt	to taste	
Pepper	to taste	
Cake flour	1 cup	Coat chicken with flour; dip in milk.
Milk	1 cup	
Parmesan cheese	1½ cups	Combine; coat chicken.
White bread crumbs	1½ cups	
Parsley, chopped	2 Tbsp.	
Vegetable oil	½ cup	Sauté garlic in oil; add chicken; sauté until golden. Remove; place in baking dish. Bake at 375F for 20 to 25 minutes.
Garlic clove, pared, crushed	1	
Fresh spinach, washed, trimmed, or frozen leaf spinach	1 lb.	Cook, uncovered, in salted boiling water until tender; drain; let cool.
Butter	1 cup	Sauté with spinach. Arrange chicken on bed of spinach. Serve.
Medium onion, pared, minced	½	
Nutmeg	to taste	

Chicken Etienne (E. Foulard)

Ingredients	2 portions	Method
Broiler-fryer chicken, 2½ lb.	1	Disjoint chicken into 4 parts; remove and discard all small inside bones. Coat chicken parts with flour; sauté in hot clarified butter until brown on all sides; discard butter.
Flour	as needed	
Butter, clarified	as needed	
Medium mushrooms, cut into quarters	12	Add; stir.
Shallots, minced	½ Tbsp.	
Garlic clove, pared, crushed	1	
Red wine	1 cup	Add; heat until reduced by half. Taste and adjust seasonings.
Tarragon leaves, fresh, minced	¼ tsp.	
Small bay leaf	1	
Sauerkraut, cooked	1 cup	Add; heat at 375F until chicken is tender.
Apple, pared, cut into wedges	1	
Parmesan cheese, grated	2 Tbsp.	

Chicken Mauna Loa (P. Schmitt)

Ingredients	4 portions	Method
Chicken breasts, 8 oz. each, boned	4	Coat chicken with egg.
Egg, lightly beaten	1	
Flour	as needed	Combine; coat chicken.
Macadamia nuts, chopped	2 oz.	
Butter	as needed	Sauté chicken until golden; cut into 1-in. strips; reserve.
Butter, melted	1 cup	Mix; cook for 3 to 5 minutes.
Flour	1 cup	
Chicken stock, warm	1 cup	Add; stir until thick.
Milk	2 cups	Add; heat to boiling. Reduce heat; simmer for 30 minutes. Strain; reserve warm.
Coconut syrup	½ cup	
Pineapple juice	¼ cup	
Pineapple, cored, cut into quarters	1	Portion reserved chicken strips into pineapple quarters. Pour 3 oz. of the reserved sauce over each.
Macadamia nuts, chopped	3 oz.	Lightly toast. Garnish pineapple quarters. Serve hot.

Breast of Chicken with Orange Sauce and Pineapple (H. Roth)

Ingredients	6 portions	Method
Chicken breasts, 5 oz. each, boned, with first wing joint left intact, skin on	6	Pat chicken dry; rub with lime juice; sprinkle with salt and pepper. Let stand for 20 minutes.
Lime juice	¼ cup	
Salt	1½ tsp.	
Black pepper, freshly ground	⅛ tsp.	
Vegetable oil	3 Tbsp.	Heat in large heavy skillet; carefully place breasts, skin side down, in hot oil; heat until brown on both sides. Remove chicken to platter. Pour oil from pan.
Dry sherry	¼ cup	Add to pan; scrape drippings from surface of pan; simmer until drippings are dissolved.
Orange juice	1 cup	Add; simmer, covered, for 5 minutes. Return chicken to pan; simmer, covered, for 10 minutes.
Chicken stock	½ cup	
Seedless raisins	¼ cup	
Ketchup	2 Tbsp.	
Lemon rind, grated	2 tsp.	
Salt	½ tsp.	
Oregano	¼ tsp.	
Fresh pineapple, cut into ¾-in. cubes	¾ cup	Add; simmer for 10 minutes or until chicken is done. Remove chicken to serving platter or casserole.
Water	2 Tbsp.	Mix; slowly add to simmering sauce until sauce is thick. Pour sauce over chicken.
Cornstarch	1 Tbsp.	
Puerto Rican rum	¼ cup	Warm in a ladle or small skillet; ignite; pour over chicken at the table before serving. Can be served with rice.

Spring Chicken Sauté Au Chablis

(P. Lenard)

Ingredients	4 portions	Method
Broiler-fryer chickens, 2½ lb. each	2	Disjoint chicken. Sprinkle chicken with seasonings as desired; coat with flour. Sauté in butter until golden.
Flour	as needed	
Butter	6 oz.	
Mushroom caps	12	Add; simmer for 3 minutes.
Shallots, minced	2 Tbsp.	
Garlic cloves, pared, crushed	1 tsp.	
Chablis	8 oz.	Add; simmer, covered, for 5 minutes.
Chicken broth	2 cups	Add; cook for about 25 minutes or until done. Remove chicken and mushrooms to casserole. Heat sauce until reduced by ⅓; strain over chicken.
Salt	to taste	
Pepper	to taste	
Mushroom caps	as needed	Garnish. Serve with buttered egg noodles and tossed salad.
Parsley, chopped	to taste	

Orange Blossom Chicken

(G. Shaffer)

Ingredients	4 portions	Method
Corn oil	½ cup	Combine thoroughly.
Cider vinegar	½ cup	
Frozen orange juice concentrate, thawed	½ cup	
Honey	½ cup	
Chili sauce	½ cup	
Worcestershire sauce	1 Tbsp., 1 tsp.	
Brown sugar	1 Tbsp.	
Dry onion flakes	1 Tbsp.	
Salt	1 tsp.	
Broiler-fryer chicken, cut into quarters	1	Pour half of the orange sauce over chicken; bake, uncovered, at 350F for 30 minutes. Pour remaining sauce over chicken; bake for 15 minutes or until fork can be inserted easily; let stand for 15 minutes. Serve on bed of lettuce with orange segments.

Chicken Sauté Beatrice

(R. Roncari)

Ingredients	6 portions	Method
Broiler-fryer chickens, 2 lb. each, cut into eighths	2	Sprinkle chicken with salt and pepper; coat with flour. Sauté in oil until brown.
Salt	to taste	
Pepper	to taste	
Flour	as needed	
Olive oil	as needed	
Large mushrooms, chopped	10	Add; simmer for several minutes.
Medium onion, pared, chopped	1	
Garlic clove, pared, crushed	1	
Medium tomatoes, peeled, chopped	6	Add; simmer until tomatoes are cooked.
White wine	2 oz.	
Parsley, chopped	1 Tbsp.	Serve on a platter; garnish with parsley.

Chicken Coriander
(J. Clary)

Ingredients	4 portions	Method
Chicken breast halves, 5 oz. each	4	Remove excess fat; place bone side down in 10-in. skillet.
Chicken stock	1 cup	Add; poach for 30 minutes. Remove chicken from broth; place on hot platter.
Dry white wine	½ cup	
Celery rib, coarsely chopped	2 oz.	
Gingerroot slice	1	
Garlic clove, pared, crushed	1	
Peanut oil	⅓ cup	Heat.
Soy sauce	2 oz.	Add. Stir with wooden spoon (watch for foaming).
Gingerroot slice, thin	1	
Coriander sprigs, chopped	8 to 10	Sprinkle over chicken; cover with peanut oil-soy sauce mixture. Serve immediately.

Chicken Cacciatore
(C. Angelo)

Ingredients	6 portions	Method
Broiler-fryer chicken, 3 lb., cut up	1	Gently cook chicken in hot oil until tender and brown.
Olive oil	½ cup	
Onion, pared, minced	1	Add; cook until translucent and golden.
Tomatoes, canned	3 cups	Add; simmer, covered tightly, for about 1 hour or until chicken is tender and tomatoes are reduced to a thick sauce.
Mushrooms, sliced	1 cup	
Green bell pepper, chopped	1	
Salt	1 Tbsp.	
Pepper	¼ Tbsp.	
Garlic clove, pared, crushed	1	
White wine	½ cup	Add during last 15 minutes of cooking.

Chicken Blanquettes
(V. Reitmaier)

Ingredients	4 portions	Method
Butter	1 cup	Sauté in heavy casserole or deep skillet for several minutes.
Onion, pared, diced	1 cup	
Carrots, pared, diced	1 cup	
Cloves	2	
Broiler-fryer chickens, 2½ lb. each, boned, skinned, cut into 1-in. cubes	2	Add; cook until chicken is seared.
Flour	as needed	Lightly coat chicken; stir.
Mushroom caps, fresh	2 cups	Add; simmer until chicken is done.
Chicken stock	2 cups	
White wine	1 cup	
Heavy cream	1 cup	Combine in separate dish. Add to chicken mixture. Serve.
Parsley, chopped	¼ cup	
Egg yolks	4	
Lemon juice	½ tsp.	

Spring House Baked Stuffed Breast of Chicken En Croûte

(W. Brun)

Ingredients	4 portions	Method
Butter or margarine Garlic cloves, pared, crushed	¼ lb. 2	Heat butter in skillet until melted; add garlic; let cool.
Onion, pared, large dice Red bell pepper, large dice Green bell pepper, large dice Scallion pieces, large dice	1 cup ¼ cup ¼ cup 3	Add; cook until about ⅔ done.
Artichoke hearts Chives, fresh or dried Parsley, fresh or dried	1 No. 303 can 2 Tbsp. 2 Tbsp.	Add; cook for several minutes.
Stuffing bread slices, chopped Filberts or walnuts	4 ¼ cup	Add; remove from heat; let cool slightly.
Egg	1	Add; reserve.
Chicken breasts, 8 oz. each, boned	4	Pound; cut into halves. Stuff halves with reserved stuffing; reserve.
Prepared pastry dough	as needed	Roll out; cut into 5-in. squares. Wrap chicken in dough.
Egg, lightly beaten	1	Brush over dough; bake at 400F until golden.

Chicken Cosmopolitan

(G. Shaffer)

Ingredients	4 portions	Method
Flour Salt Black pepper	½ cup 1 tsp. ¼ tsp.	Combine.
Broiler-fryer chicken, 3½ lb., cut into parts	1	Coat with flour mixture. Let stand for 10 minutes.
Corn oil	½ cup	Heat in skillet over medium heat. Add chicken; heat until brown on all sides. Remove chicken; place in baking pan. Reduce heat; pour off all but 2 Tbsp. of the oil.
Green bell pepper, cut into strips Onion, pared, sliced	½ cup ½ cup	Add to pan; sauté until limp.
Chicken stock Green olives, pimento-stuffed Flour Oregano	2 cups ½ cup 1 Tbsp. 1 tsp.	Add; cook, stirring constantly, until mixture thickens slightly.
Raisins Capers, drained	½ cup 2 oz.	Add; pour over chicken. Bake, covered, at 350F, basting every 15 minutes, for about 45 minutes or until fork can be inserted easily into chicken.
Dry white wine	½ cup	Add during last 15 minutes.

Chicken Divan

(O. Sommer)

Ingredients	10 portions	Method
Flour Salt White pepper Garlic powder	10 oz. 1 tsp. ½ tsp. ⅛ tsp.	Mix; reserve.
Whole milk Egg, well beaten	1 cup 1	Mix; reserve.
Chicken breasts, 8 oz. each, skinned, boned, split	5	Coat with reserved flour mixture; then dip into reserved egg mixture; then coat with flour mixture. Deep-fry at 375F for 6 minutes; reserve warm.
Hot water Chicken base	2 qt. 3 oz.	Mix; heat to boiling.
Butter Onion, pared, minced	4 oz. 2 oz.	Sauté onion in separate pan until translucent.
Flour	4 oz.	Add; combine thoroughly. Cook for 2 minutes. Add to boiling chicken stock; stir rapidly until thick.
Mushrooms, canned, sliced Red bell peppers, diced Prepared mustard Worcestershire sauce Salt White pepper	8 oz. 2 oz. 3 Tbsp. 1 Tbsp. 1 tsp. ¼ tsp.	Add; combine thoroughly. Remove from heat.
Broccoli spears, cooked crisp-tender, warm	2 lb.	Arrange chicken and broccoli on plates. Top each portion with 3 oz. of the sauce.
Orange, thinly sliced Parsley sprigs	1 10	Garnish.

Chicken Alfredo with Fettuccine

(R. Soeder)

Ingredients	4 portions	Method
Chicken breasts, 5 oz. each, boned Salt Pepper Flour Eggs, beaten Vegetable oil	4 ½ tsp. ½ tsp. 1 cup 3 1 cup	Sprinkle chicken with salt and pepper; coat with flour; dip in eggs. Cook in hot oil until golden on both sides. Remove to greased pan. Bake at 450F for 10 to 15 minutes.
Flour Butter or margarine, melted	1 cup 2 Tbsp.	Mix well; cook over low heat for 10 to 15 minutes.
Milk Cheese, grated Chicken base	1 qt. ¾ cup ½ tsp.	Add slowly, stirring constantly, until sauce is thick.
Fettuccine, cooked, drained, warm	1 lb.	Toss lightly with some of the cream sauce.
Broccoli spears, cooked, drained	1 lb.	Place chicken over fettuccine; top with broccoli and more of the cream sauce.
Parsley, chopped	½ tsp.	Garnish; serve.

Chicken Manuel

(J. Douglas)

Ingredients	1 portion	Method
Chicken half, boned	1	Sprinkle chicken with seasonings.
Salt	to taste	
Black pepper	to taste	
Chorizo sausage	2 oz.	Stuff chorizo and cheese into pepper. Place pepper in center of chicken; fold chicken over to form an envelope.
Monterey Jack cheese	1 oz.	
Hot green pepper, seeded, blanched	½	
Egg, lightly beaten	1	Dip chicken in egg; then in flour; then in bread crumbs. Deep-fry at 350F until brown. Bake at 350F until done.
Flour	as needed	
Bread crumbs	as needed	
Oil	as needed	
Sauce Manuel	recipe follows	Serve with.

Sauce Manuel

(J. Douglas)

Ingredients	1 portion	Method
Tomato sauce, purée or paste	¼ cup	Combine in saucepan; stir well.
White wine	¼ cup	
Worcestershire sauce	1 tsp.	
Dijon-style mustard	½ tsp.	
Salt	to taste	
Pepper	to taste	
Chicken broth	2 cups	Add.
Cornstarch	as needed	Mix; add to thicken. Simmer, stirring constantly, for 1 to 2 minutes. Pour over Chicken Manual: serve.
Water, cold	as needed	

Chicken and Shrimp Veronique

(R. Morgan)

Ingredients	4 portions	Method
Colossal shrimp, U-15, in shells	8	Peel shrimp, leaving tails on. Sprinkle with salt, pepper, butter and lemon juice as desired. Bake at 350F for 10 minutes; reserve.
Salt	to taste	
Pepper	to taste	
Butter, melted	to taste	
Lemon juice	to taste	
Chicken breasts, 7 oz. each, boned, flattened	4	Sprinkle chicken with salt and pepper; dust with flour; sauté in clarified butter until golden.
Salt	to taste	
Pepper	to taste	
Flour	as needed	
Butter, clarified	as needed	
Chablis or sauterne	½ cup	Add; ignite to burn off alcohol.
Heavy cream	1 cup	Add; bake at 350F for 15 minutes. Place a chicken breast in the center of each serving plate. Place 2 of the reserved shrimp on each breast.
Seedless white grapes	1 cup	Add to chicken pan; heat for 1 minute. Spoon grapes and sauce over chicken and shrimp.
Parsley, chopped	2 Tbsp.	Sprinkle on top. Can be served with rice pilaf.

POULTRY

Shredded Turkey Milwaukee **(F. Sonnenschmidt)**

Ingredients	1 portion	Method
Bacon, julienne	2 oz.	Sauté; remove from pan; reserve. Drain fat from pan.
Butter	2 Tbsp.	Add to pan; heat.
Turkey breast, shredded Salt	½ cup to taste	Sprinkle turkey with salt; sauté. Remove; reserve warm.
Red bell peppers, julienne Green bell peppers, julienne	3 Tbsp. 3 Tbsp.	Add; sauté.
Ketchup Garlic clove, pared, crushed	2 Tbsp. ½	Add; cook for 3 minutes.
Flour	as needed	Lightly coat peppers.
Beer	½ cup	Add; bring to boil; simmer for 1 minute.
Tomato, blanched, peeled, seeded, diced Kosher pickles, julienne Scallions, sliced Paprika Salt Pepper	1 2 oz. 1 tsp. 1 tsp. to taste to taste	Add with reserved turkey and bacon. Heat; adjust seasonings; serve.

Capon in Beer Sauce **(D. Barnikel)**

Ingredients	10-12 portions	Method
Pilsener or dark imported beer, 12-oz. bottles Medium onions, pared, chopped Large carrot, pared, chopped Shallots, chopped Bouquet garni Juniper berries	2 2 1 2 1 8	Combine for a marinade.
Capon, 5 to 6 lb.	1	Place in marinade; marinate in refrigerator for 30 hours. Remove from marinade; pat dry with paper toweling. Strain marinade; reserve.
Oil	2½ oz.	Sauté capon in oil until golden on all sides.
Gin	¼ cup	Pour over capon; flambé.
Flour	1 Tbsp.	Sprinkle over capon. Add just enough of the reserved marinade to cover the capon; simmer for 25 minutes or until capon is done.
Sugar Salt Pepper	to taste to taste to taste	Add.
Heavy cream Butter	3 Tbsp. 1 oz.	Mix; stir into sauce just before serving.

Outdoor Paella (G. Corelli)

Ingredients	10 portions	Method
Broiler-fryer chicken, 4 lb.	1	Cut each chicken leg into 2 pieces; cut each breast into 3 pieces. Grill over high heat or broil for 4 to 5 minutes until light brown. Place in 12x20x3-in. aluminum pan.
Chorizo sausage	1 lb., 4 oz.	Cut into 2-in. links (about 2 oz. each); place in pan with chicken.
Italian sausage	1 lb., 4 oz.	
Pimentos	1 12-oz. can	Combine; arrange evenly over chicken and sausage.
Onions, pared, diced	1⅓ cups	
Green bell pepper, diced	1⅓ cups	
Olive oil	⅓ cup	
Capers	¼ cup	
Garlic cloves, pared, crushed	4	
Oregano	2 tsp.	
Black pepper	2 tsp.	
Coriander	⅓ tsp.	
White rice, uncooked	1 qt.	Pour evenly over mixture.
Chicken stock	2 qt.	Pour evenly over mixture.
Littleneck clams, in shell	3 qt.	Add; cover pan tightly with aluminum foil. Punch 2 holes with fork in cover. Cook over medium heat in covered grill or in moderate oven for about 1 hour or until all liquid is absorbed by rice.
Mussels, in shell	2 qt., 1 cup	

Chicken Fontina (M. Piccinino)

Ingredients	10 portions	Method
Chicken breasts, 7 oz. each, boned, skinned, pounded ¼-in. thick	5	Cut in half.
Italian bread crumbs	6½ oz.	Combine in plastic bag; add breasts; shake until well coated; shake off excess.
Paprika	to taste	
Salt	to taste	
Pepper	to taste	
Butter	5 oz.	Heat in large skillet until bubbly. Sauté chicken for 2 or 3 minutes on each side (do not overcook). Drain on paper toweling; reserve warm. Drain half of the pan drippings; reserve remaining half.
Olive oil	1 oz.	
Madeira	5 oz.	Add to reserved drippings, scraping bottom of skillet to loosen any brown pieces.
Lemon, juice of	1	Add; heat briefly. Return reserved chicken to skillet; heat until sauce is thick.
Parsley, minced	5 oz.	Add; stir in. Remove chicken to platter.
Capers	2½ oz.	
Fontina cheese, thinly sliced	as desired	Place cheese slices over chicken; spoon some of the sauce over the cheese. Sprinkle with parsley.
Parsley, minced	as desired	

Chicken Sauté Marengo A La Dubois
(D. Chen)

Ingredients	8 portions	Method
Broiler-fryer chickens, 5 lb. each	2	Disjoint chicken into 4 parts; remove and discard backbone. Wash chicken; coat with flour.
Flour	2 Tbsp.	
Oil	as needed	Heat in pan; sauté chicken until brown. Remove from pan; reserve.
Water	1½ cups	Add to pan; combine thoroughly.
White wine	1 cup	
Flour	4 Tbsp.	
Butter or margarine	2 Tbsp.	
Tomato purée	1 Tbsp.	
Bouquet garni	1	
Garlic clove, pared, crushed	1	
Worcestershire sauce	5 dashes	Add with reserved chicken; heat to boiling; remove from heat. Bake at 375F for about 20 minutes. Remove chicken; strain sauce into another pan.
Hot pepper sauce	4 dashes	
Salt	to taste	
Pepper	to taste	
Mushrooms	8 oz.	Add to pan; then add chicken. Heat to boiling; boil for several minutes. Remove from heat; taste and adjust seasonings and thickness of sauce. Arrange chicken on platter. Pour sauce over.
Eggs, fried	8	Place eggs on top of sauce; top with onion rings.
French-fried onion rings	1 lb.	

Stuffed Boneless Chicken Legs
(G. Corelli)

Ingredients	7 portions	Method
Butter	2 Tbsp.	Sauté until onion is light brown.
Celery, diced	½ cup	
Onion, pared, diced	¼ cup	
Garlic cloves, pared, crushed	2	
Ham, diced	12 oz.	Add; cook for 4 to 5 minutes.
Frozen spinach, chopped	5 oz.	
Fresh chives, chopped	⅛ cup	
Black pepper	¼ tsp.	
Swiss cheese, diced	1 oz.	Add; cook for 2 to 3 minutes or until cheese is melted and thoroughly combined. Remove from heat; let cool.
Cheddar cheese, diced	1 oz.	
Medium egg, beaten	1	
Chicken legs, 5 to 6 oz. each, boned	7	Portion stuffing evenly into chicken legs; press into cavity where bone was removed; place remaining stuffing in thigh. Place, skin side up, on lightly buttered sheet pan or in shallow casserole.
Butter, melted	as needed	Brush lightly over chicken; sprinkle with seasonings as desired.
Bread crumbs	as needed	Sprinkle over chicken. Bake at 350F for 50 to 60 minutes or until tender. Arrange on platter or serve in casserole.
Lemon, juice of	1	Garnish; serve immediately.
Chives, chopped	to taste	

Chicken Breast Imperial Garden

(K. Elmer)

Ingredients	4 portions	Method
Chicken breasts, 8 oz. each, boned	4	Carefully cut chicken without tearing the skin into bite-size pieces about 1 in. square (9 to 10 pieces per breast).
Butter	4 oz.	Heat in sauté pan; add chicken; sauté for about 3 minutes.
Zucchini, cut into half-moon slices, 1 in. in diameter and ¼-in. thick	8 oz.	Add; sauté for about 3 minutes or until chicken is brown and vegetables are crisp-tender.
Fresh mushrooms, cut into quarters	8 oz.	
Carrot sticks, ⅛ in. x 1½ in.	4 oz.	
Lemons	2	Squeeze over chicken mixture; shake pan. Taste and adjust seasonings.
Soy sauce	¼ cup	Add; combine thoroughly; remove from heat.
Scallions, minced	1 Tbsp., 1 tsp.	Garnish; serve.

Riced Turkey Vienna Style

(F. Sonnenschmidt)

Ingredients	4 portions	Method
Vegetable oil	1 Tbsp.	Heat in saucepan.
Turkey, dark meat, cut into 1-in. dice	12 oz.	Add; quickly heat until brown.
Water or stock, heated	3½ cups	Add; heat to boiling. Bake, covered, at 350F until done. Remove from oven. Taste and adjust seasonings.
Rice, uncooked	1¾ cups	
Onion, pared, small dice	½ cup	
Tomato paste or ketchup	1 Tbsp.	
Salt	to taste	
Pepper	to taste	
Parmesan cheese, freshly grated	¼ cup	Fold in.
Butter	¼ cup	

Menehune Chicken

(E. Leong)

Ingredients	6 portions	Method
Soy sauce	1 cup	Combine.
Green onions, minced	¾ cup	
Sugar	⅓ cup	
Vegetable oil	1 Tbsp.	
Ground ginger or 1 Tbsp. grated, pared fresh gingerroot	1½ tsp.	
Garlic clove, pared, crushed	1	
Chicken wings	24	Disjoint chicken wings; remove and discard tips. Add; marinate for 30 minutes. Remove chicken; reserve marinade. Place chicken in single layer in shallow baking pan. Bake, uncovered, at 350F for 15 minutes; turn chicken; baste with reserved marinade; bake for 15 minutes.

Chicken Velouté Supreme   (B. Bardy)

Ingredients	16 portions	Method
Butter	2 oz.	Heat butter in saucepan until melted; add flour; cook
Flour	2 oz.	(do not brown).
Chicken stock	1 qt.	Add; heat to boiling. Reduce heat; simmer for 30
Lemon juice	1 tsp.	minutes; strain.
White wine	2 oz.	
Heavy cream, hot	4 oz.	Add.
Salt	to taste	
White pepper	to taste	

Roast Duckling with Lychee Nuts   (V. Reitmaier)

Ingredients	4 portions	Method
Ducks, 4 lb. each	2	Roast duck, breast up, on rack at 450F for 20 minutes until skin is lightly brown. Pour off excess fat from pan; discard. Reduce heat to 350F. Turn duck, breast side down, and roast for 30 minutes more. Turn duck breast side up again; continue cooking for 30 minutes or until crisp and brown. Pour 1 cup of drippings from duck roasting pan into saucepan.
Flour	½ cup	Add to duck drippings. Place over low heat; stir until thick.
Lychee nuts	2 29-oz. cans	Drain. Reserve juice and nuts. Stir juice into duck drippings until smooth and well-blended.
Demiglace	1 cup	Add. Stir to blend. Bring to boil, stirring constantly.
Sweet port	½ cup	Reduce heat; simmer for 20 minutes. Remove from
Sugar syrup, boiled to 180F	¼ cup	heat; adjust seasonings; strain. To serve: split duck in
Lemons, chopped	2	half; remove rib bones. Place duck skin side up. Sprinkle reserved lychee nuts on top. Pour sauce over duck. Accompany with wild rice and sautéed pea pods.

Chicken Ricardo   (J. Clary)

Ingredients	4 portions	Method
Chicken breast halves, 5 oz. each, skinned, boned	4	Remove excess fat.
Flour	¼ cup	Combine; lightly coat chicken.
Salt	1½ tsp.	
Pepper	½ tsp.	
Garlic powder	½ tsp.	
Peanut oil	as needed	Coat a 10-in. skillet. Add chicken; cook until brown on both sides.
Chablis	2 oz.	Deglaze.
Tomato slices	8	Alternately layer 2 of the tomato slices and 2 of the
Avocado slices	8	avocado slices on each chicken breast.
Cheddar cheese, shredded	1½ oz.	Sprinkle over tops; heat in broiler for 1 to 2 minutes; serve hot.

Chicken Breasts Espagnola
(J. Lucero)

Ingredients	4 portions	Method
Chicken breasts, boned	4	Combine; poach in water to cover for 30 to 40 minutes. Reserve hot.
Onion, pared, chopped	¼ cup	
Celery, chopped	¼ cup	
Salt	as needed	
Lard	1 tsp.	Melt.
Flour	1½ tsp.	Add; cook until golden.
Chili powder, mild	2 tsp.	Add; heat lightly.
Stock from poaching liquid	1 cup	Add; simmer for 10 minutes; keep hot. Slice reserved chicken breasts on an angle into thirds.
Chili powder, mild	2 tsp.	
Garlic clove, pared, crushed	½	
Cumin	to taste	
Avocados, pared, cut in half, sliced into wedges	2	Place with chicken on a baking sheet or in a casserole. Alternate 3 wedges between 3 chicken pieces. Top with some of the chili sauce.
American cheese slices, cut in half	4	Place on top of chicken and avocado; top with remaining sauce. Bake at 350F until cheese is slightly melted. Serve hot.

Chicken Pie with Sweet Potato Crust
(W. O'Neill)

Ingredients	6-8 portions	Method
Flour, sifted	1 cup	Combine; sift once. Reserve.
Baking powder	1 tsp.	
Salt	½ tsp.	
Sweet potatoes, cooked, mashed	1 cup	Mix well. Add reserved flour; blend well. Roll to ¼-in. thickness.
Butter or margarine, melted	⅓ cup	
Egg, well beaten	1	
Chicken meat, cooked, diced	3 cups	Arrange in layers in casserole. Reserve.
Carrots, cooked, diced	1 cup	
Small white onions, cooked	6	
Parsley, chopped	1 Tbsp.	
Evaporated milk	1 cup	Mix in bowl.
Chicken broth	1 cup	
Flour	2 Tbsp.	Add slowly, blending well. Cook until thick, stirring constantly. Pour over chicken and vegetables in casserole. Cover with sweet potato crust and seal. Bake at 350F for 40 minutes or until chicken mixture is bubbly and crust is golden.
Salt	1 tsp.	

Roast Duckling A L'Orange

(J. Mannke)

Ingredients	4 portions	Method
Ducklings	2	Trim excess fat at base of tail and inside; chop giblets; reserve.
Salt Rosemary Black pepper	1 tsp. ½ tsp. ½ tsp.	Sprinkle inside and outside of ducklings with seasonings. Place ducklings and reserved giblets in pan. Roast at 450F, basting occasionally, for 1½ hours. Remove; reserve warm. Pour off all but about 2 Tbsp. of fat from pan.
Celery rib, chopped Small carrot, pared, chopped Small onion, pared, chopped	1 1 1	Add; sauté, stirring constantly, for 10 minutes.
Flour Water, hot	2 Tbsp. 3 cups	Dust flour over vegetable mixture; add hot water. Boil for 15 minutes; strain; reserve.
Sugar Butter	3 Tbsp. 1 Tbsp.	Heat in saucepan until melted.
Orange, peeled, cut into wedges Cider vinegar	1 ½ cup	Add; heat to boiling.
Orange juice English mustard Cloves	1 cup 1 tsp. 3	Add with reserved duck sauce; boil for 5 minutes; strain.
Orange-flavored liqueur	½ cup	Add; serve over reserved ducklings.

Chicken Piccata with Linguine

(R. Soeder)

Ingredients	4 portions	Method
Linguine	1 lb.	Cook linguine according to package directions; drain; reserve.
Chicken breasts, 5 oz. each, boned Flour	4 1 cup	Lightly coat chicken.
Eggs, beaten Parmesan cheese, grated	3 1½ Tbsp.	Combine; coat chicken.
Olive oil	¾ cup	Heat chicken until brown on both sides. Bake at 400F for about 15 minutes; reserve.
Olive oil Garlic cloves, pared, chopped	¼ cup 2	Sauté.
Zucchini, sliced Tomatoes, chopped Mushrooms, chopped Salt Pepper Basil	1 cup 8 oz. 4 oz. to taste to taste to taste	Add; cook slowly for about 5 minutes. Pour half into large bowl; reserve remaining half.
Cheese, grated	1½ Tbsp.	Add with reserved linguine; toss lightly. Transfer to serving plate; top with reserved chicken; cover with reserved sauce.
Parsley, chopped	3 Tbsp.	Sprinkle over chicken.

Roast Goose with Potato Onion Stuffing   (J. De Beus)

Ingredients	6 portions	Method
Goose	1	Clean goose; pat dry. Rub with lemon and salt.
Lemon halves	as needed	
Salt	as needed	
Potatoes, boiled, pared, chopped	1 lb.	Combine; stuff goose; tie legs together. Place, breast side up, on rack in roasting pan.
Bread crumbs	1 cup	
Medium onion, pared, minced	1	
Celery leaves	½ cup	
Parsley, chopped	¼ cup	
Eggs, lightly beaten	2	
Salt	1½ tsp.	
Sage	1 tsp.	
Chives, chopped	to taste	
Basil	to taste	
Celery rib, leaves on	1	Add to pan. Roast at 350F 20 minutes for every pound. When skin is brown and crisp, prick skin around wings and legs to release fat. Place on heated platter.
Garlic clove, pared, whole	1	
Watercress	as needed	Garnish. Can be served with applesauce.

Turkey Cutlet Normandy Style   (F. Sonnenschmidt)

Ingredients	4 portions	Method
Butter	1 Tbsp.	Heat in skillet.
Oil	1 Tbsp.	
Turkey cutlets, 1 to 1½ oz. each	4	Add; sauté for 2 minutes on each side.
Apple, pared, sliced lengthwise	1	Add; sauté. Remove cutlets from pan; reserve on warm plate. Drain excess fat from skillet.
Crème fraîse or sour cream	¼ cup, 2 Tbsp.	Add; heat (do not boil). Serve sautéed cutlets and apples over sauce.

Chicken Cashew Sauté   (E. Leong)

Ingredients	4 portions	Method
Chicken breasts, boned, skinned, cut into ½-in. cubes	2	Sprinkle sake and gingerroot over chicken. Coat with cornstarch. Reserve.
Sake or dry white wine	1 tsp.	
Gingerroot, fresh, grated	1 tsp.	
Cornstarch	1 Tbsp.	
Cashew nuts	2 Tbsp.	Sauté nuts over low heat until golden. Remove from pan. Reserve.
Vegetable oil	1 Tbsp.	
Vegetable oil	2 Tbsp.	Add to pan; heat. Sauté reserved chicken for about 5 minutes or until cooked.
Soy sauce	2 Tbsp.	Add.
Sake or dry white wine	1 Tbsp.	
Sugar	to taste	
Cornstarch	½ tsp.	Dissolve cornstarch in water; add; cook until thick. Remove from heat; stir. Add reserved nuts. Can be served hot with rice.
Water	1 Tbsp.	

Chicken Supremes Swedish Style
(R. Werth)

Ingredients	6 portions	Method
Chicken breasts, boned	6	Moisten each breast with a little of the lemon juice; sprinkle each with salt and pepper.
Lemon juice	as needed	
Salt	to taste	
Pepper	to taste	
Butter, clarified	as needed	Heat; sauté chicken until golden on both sides; reserve warm.
Puff pastry	1 lb., 8 oz.	Roll out into 12 4x6-in. rectangles. Place 1 breast on each rectangle.
Asparagus spears, large, cooked	12	Place 2 of the asparagus spears on each breast; place 2 of the shrimp 'horseback' on the spears. Cover with another rectangle; seal, leaving slight opening so asparagus and shrimp can be seen.
Shrimp, 21-25, peeled, deveined, cooked	12	
Eggs, lightly beaten	2	Brush over pastry. Bake at 375F until pastry is golden.
Sauce Choron	recipe follows	Remove chicken to platter; serve with Sauce Choron.

Sauce Choron
(R. Werth)

Ingredients	1½ pt.	Method
Egg yolks	6	Place in stainless steel bowl; beat well. Hold bowl over hot water bath and continue to beat until eggs are thickened and creamy. Remove bowl from heat.
Cold water	1 oz.	
Butter, clarified	1½ lb.	Using ladle, slowly and gradually beat butter into yolks. Add drop by drop at first, then in steady stream.
Lemon, juice of	1	Add when all butter has been added.
Cayenne pepper	to taste	Add. Serve over chicken breasts.
Salt	to taste	
Minced onions	1 oz.	
Peppercorn, crushed	½ tsp.	
Tarragon vinegar	½ cup	
Tomato purée	1 Tbsp.	

Chicken Argento
(J. Nargi)

Ingredients	1-2 portions	Method
Broiler-fryer chicken	½	Arrange on large sheet of aluminum foil.
Onion, pared, sliced	½	
Carrot sticks	4	
Celery sticks	2	
Potato, pared, cut into ½-in.-thick sticks	¼	
Bay leaves	2	
Rosemary	to taste	Sprinkle over chicken. Tightly seal foil around chicken and vegetables. Bake at 375F for 45 minutes. Serve hot.
Salt	to taste	
Pepper	to taste	
White wine	to taste	

Chicken Supreme A La Florentine (K. Sayre)

Ingredients	6 portions	Method
Chicken breasts, boned, skinned, split	6	Sprinkle chicken with salt and pepper.
Salt	¾ tsp.	
White pepper	⅛ tsp.	
Butter	3 Tbsp.	Heat over medium heat. Add chicken. Sauté, covered, for 3 to 4 minutes on each side or until just done. Remove from pan; reserve warm.
Butter	2 Tbsp.	Heat in heavy pan until melted.
Spinach, fresh, washed, stemmed, drained	2 lb., 8 oz.	Add; cook, covered, over medium heat, stirring occasionally, until spinach is wilted and tender. Portion spinach with slotted spoon into 6 individual casseroles; arrange reserved chicken on spinach beds.
Salt	½ tsp.	
Pepper	¼ tsp.	
Mozzarella cheese slices, thin	6	Place over chicken; heat in broiler until brown. Serve hot.
Parmesan cheese, grated	3 tsp.	

Sautéed Chicken with Red Pepper (F. Buck)

Ingredients	10 portions	Method
Broiler-fryer chickens, cut into quarters	5	Sprinkle salt over chicken; heat chicken in oil until brown. Remove chicken; reserve.
Salt	to taste	
Vegetable oil	as needed	
Onions, pared, chopped	14 oz.	Add to pan; sauté.
Bacon, cured, diced	3½ oz.	
Tomato pulp	1 cup	Add; lightly sauté. Spread over reserved chicken.
Garlic, pared, chopped	10 oz.	
Hungarian red peppers, diced	3 oz.	
Beef broth	1 qt.	Pour over chicken; steam for 25 minutes. Remove chicken; reserve.
Flour	1½ oz.	Mix; add. Heat until reduced to desired consistency. Strain over reserved chicken.
Heavy cream	1 cup	

BEEF

Academy chefs reflect America's love affair with beef: (clockwise from top) Braised Short Ribs, Almond Beef Steak and Sliced Beef Tenderloin a la Deutsch.

Good beef has a fresh red color, a smooth covering of brittle creamy fat and small streaks of fat distributed through the lean. In other words, it is well-marbled with fat. The lean is firm, fine-grained and velvety. The bones in young beef are porous and red, in older animals they are white and flinty.

The purpose of meat inspection is to protect the consumer. According to federal law, meat sold between states and subject to interstate commerce regulations must be inspected. This service is an assurance that the meat is from healthy animals slaughtered under sanitary conditions and is safe for consumption at the time of inspection.

Inspected meat is identified with a round, purple federal inspection stamp. The stamping is done with a safe purple vegetable dye on each wholesale cut. Because of the mechanized method of stamping, the stamp might not appear on all retail cuts. It is not necessary to cut the stamp off before cooking.

The grading of meat is not required by law, but most meat packers prefer to sell graded meat. The U.S. Department of Agriculture has set standards for different grades of meat. The meat grades indicate the quality of the meat while inspection indicates its wholesomeness.

Beef is graded for two factors: quality and cutability. Quality refers to the proportion of meat to bone, the degree of marbling in the lean, the firmness in texture and the normal color. Cutability refers to the proportion of edible meat: a greater amount of muscle in relation to a smaller layer of external fat. Beef graded for quality and cutability helps one select high-quality beef without excess fat.

In the United States, the three grades of beef found in the consumer marketplace are prime, choice and good. These are judged according to breed, age, state of fattening and sex.

Veal is meat from very young milk-fed calves, usually not over 12 weeks of age at the time of slaughter. It is light grayish pink in color. The meat is very fine-grained, velvety and fairly firm, with little surface fat and no marbling. The fat is clear, firm and white, and the bones are porous and red. —*Harry H. Hoffstadt*

Almond Beef Steak (R. Kinney)

Ingredients	1 portion	Method
Ground beef	8 oz.	Form into oval steak 1-in. thick; broil to desired doneness.
Mushrooms, sliced	1 oz.	Sauté.
Celery, sliced	½ oz.	
Bamboo shoots, sliced	½ oz.	
Butter	as needed	
Shallots, pared	¼ oz.	Add; sauté.
Almonds, sliced	¼ oz.	
Brown sauce	2 oz.	Add. Place steak in center of hot dinner plate; cover with vegetable sauce.

Diabetic Beef Stew (M. Farano)

Ingredients	2 portions	Method
Lean beef, cubed	4 oz.	Brown until partly cooked.
Lard	2 tsp.	
Water	2 cups	Add; simmer slowly until meat is tender.
Salt	to taste	
Pepper	to taste	
Celery, chopped	½ cup	Add.
Carrots, medium dice	½ cup	
Onion, pared, chopped	½ cup	Add; simmer slowly until tender. Reduce liquid slightly.
Green peppers, medium dice	½ cup	
Small potatoes, pared, medium dice	2	
Mushrooms, sliced	½ cup	Add just before serving.

Sliced Beef Tenderloin a la Deutsch   (H. Hoffstadt)

Ingredients	8 portions	Method
Large Spanish onion, sliced	1	Sauté in small amount of oil until light brown.
Oil	as needed	
Garlic cloves, pared, finely diced	2	Add; sauté slightly.
Shallots, pared, finely diced	½ cup	
Large green pepper, cut in squares	2	Add; sauté until half done.
Mushrooms, sliced	½ lb.	
Brown gravy	½ cup	Add; let simmer slowly.
Large tomatoes, medium dice	3	
Beef tenderloin tips	3 lb.	Slice in long strips; sauté in hot skillet until brown.
Red wine	¼ cup	Add; ignite. Combine with vegetable mixture; simmer slowly.
Potatoes, pared, boiled	4	Slice in medallions; roast in butter on both sides until brown. Place beef and vegetables in silver tray. Garnish with chopped parsley and watercress. Arrange potato medallions along edge of tray.
Butter	as needed	

Oven Braised Short Ribs of Beef   (H. Carruthers)

Ingredients	6 portions	Method
Short ribs, trimmed, 8-10 oz. each	3½ lb.	Tie ends on each rib; arrange ribs bone side down; cook at 400F for 1 hour. Remove from oven; take ribs out of pan and reserve. Place roast pan over open burner.
Flour	as needed	Mix well into drippings.
Water or beef stock, boiling	6 cups	Add gradually while stirring; heat to boiling.
Garlic clove, pared, chopped	1	Add; return ribs to pan. Cover; place in oven. Reduce temperature to 350F, stirring occasionally. Continue cooking until meat and vegetables are tender, for 2 hours.
Onion, pared, coarsely chopped	1 cup	
Carrots, ¾-in. dice	1 cup	
Celery, ¾-in. dice	1 cup	
Tomato purée	1 cup	
Salt	1 Tbsp.	
Pepper	½ tsp.	
Cloves	6	Insert a clove in 6 of onions. Gently boil in slightly salted water until tender. Drain; reserve water.
Tiny white onions	12	
Baby carrots	12	Steam until tender.
Frozen green peas	¾ cup	Blanch; drain immediately.
Cornstarch, dissolved in cold water	1 Tbsp.	Heat 1 cup reserved water to boiling; stir in cornstarch. Use as glaze for onions and carrots. Serve with ribs.

Filet Mignon Chasseur

(V. Reitmaier)

Ingredients	4 portions	Method
Beef fillets, 8 oz. each, seasoned with salt and pepper	4	Heat oil in skillet; sauté fillets until brown on all sides. Remove fillets; discard oil.
Oil	¼ cup	
Butter	¼ cup	Add to skillet; melt.
Shallots, pared, minced	2 Tbsp.	Add; sauté.
Mushrooms, sliced	2 cups	
White wine	½ cup	Add; simmer until combined; adjust seasoning and thickness.
Demiglace	1 cup	
Glace de viande	3 Tbsp.	
Toasted rounds, slightly smaller than diameter of fillets	4	Place fillets on toast rounds; top with sauce.

Beef and Chicken Stir Fry

(K. Loos)

Ingredients	4 portions	Method
Sesame oil	¼ cup	Sauté.
Garlic, pared, minced	1 tsp.	
Sirloin of beef, julienne	12 oz.	Add; sauté quickly; do not overcook.
Chicken, boned, julienne	12 oz.	
Mushroom, sliced	4 oz.	Add; cook quickly.
Green pepper, julienne	4 oz.	
Green onions, julienne	4 oz.	
Carrot, julienne	4 oz.	
Celery, julienne	4 oz.	
Ketchup	8 oz.	Combine; add and stir well. Adjust seasonings. Serve quickly with steamed rice.
Curry powder	4 tsp.	

Beef Stew Burgundy

(V. Reitmaier)

Ingredients	8 portions	Method
Oil	1 cup	Heat in heavy casserole or skillet. Add onion and garlic; sauté for a few minutes.
Onions, pared, small dice	1 lb.	
Garlic, pared, minced	1 Tbsp.	
Beef, cut in 1-in. x 1-in. cubes, lean	2 lb.	Stir in until seared.
Salt	to taste	Season.
Peppercorns, crushed	to taste	
Flour	½ cup	Add; stir constantly.
Tomato purée	1 cup	
Burgundy	2 cups	
Celery, medium dice	½ lb.	Add when meat is cooked; heat to boiling. Adjust seasonings.
Carrots, medium dice	½ lb.	
Beef stock	4 cups	
Fresh parsley, chopped	3 Tbsp.	Sprinkle over meat. Garnish with small sautéed onions and pared boiled potatoes.

Lord Buckingham Filet   (A. Dumancas)

Ingredients	4 portions	Method
Beef tenderloin Flour	1 lb., 8 oz. as needed	Cut into 3 oz. medallions; flatten. Dust with flour.
Butter, clarified	4 oz.	Sauté meat in butter; place on platter; reserve warm.
Onion, pared, minced Green bell pepper, minced Mushrooms, minced	½ cup ½ cup ½ cup	Add; sauté.
Curry powder Salt Pepper	1 tsp. pinch pinch	Season meat.
Beef stock Tomato, medium dice Heavy cream Dry sherry	1 cup 1 1 cup 4 oz.	Add; reduce sauce slightly. Spoon sauce and vegetables over tenderloin.

Stuffed Mushrooms   (J. Greenwalt)

Ingredients	4 portions	Method
Large mushrooms, 2-2½-in. diameter	8	Wash; remove stems; reserve.
Ground chuck Onion, pared, finely chopped Celery, finely chopped Coarse black pepper Salt Prepared steak sauce	1 lb. ¼ cup ¼ cup 1 tsp. 1 tsp. 3 Tbsp.	Combine; mix well. Split in 8 equal portions. Pack meat mixture into mushroom, forming into a ball shape under mushroom. Place in baking dish meat down. Bake at 400F for 20 minutes or until desired doneness. Remove from baking dish.
Sour cream	1 cup	Add to remaining meat juices. Heat but do not boil. Pour over mushroom; serve with rice.

Entrecote Au Poivre Flambé   (L. Schaeli)

Ingredients	2 portions	Method

Strip loin steak, 6 oz. each,
  trimmed, pounded with
  crushed black peppercorns.
	2	Cook as desired on grill or in skillet; reserve.

Medium oysters, open Champagne Shallots, pared, chopped	12 5-6 oz. 1 Tbsp.	Poach oysters in champagne with shallots and seasoning. Remove oysters. Reduce sauce by half.
Heavy cream Butter	5-6 oz. 3-4 oz.	Add.
Shallots, pared, chopped Garlic, pared, minced	2 oz. ½ oz.	Sauté until transparent.
Cognac	2 oz.	Add precooked steaks to skillet; flame with cognac.
Glace de viande Seasoning salt Black peppercorns, crushed	2-3 oz. to taste to taste	Add; season. Keep turning steaks until sauce is mixed well and hot. Serve steaks on hot plates with oysters on top. Spoon champagne sauce over.

Fillet of Veal Roof Restaurant (R. Cortello)

Ingredients	8 portions	Method
Veal fillets, 3 oz. each	8	Sauté until browned and three-quarters cooked.
Butter	6-8 Tbsp.	
Salt	to taste	Season to taste. Remove veal; reserve warm.
Pepper	to taste	
Mushroom caps, sliced thinly	18	Sauté in pan drippings for a few minutes.
Shallots, pared, chopped	3-4 Tbsp.	
Dry sherry	8 Tbsp.	Add; cook while stirring constantly until reduced by half.
Prepared crepes	8	Spoon even part of mushroom and shallot mixture on one side of each crêpe. Place fillet on top; close pancake very carefully. Turn over; place on a buttered sheet pan.
Butter, melted	as needed	Brush over each pancake.
Gruyère cheese, grated	8 Tbsp.	Sprinkle over each pancake. Place in preheated 400F oven for 5-7 minutes.

Beefsteak in Sour Cream Hungarian Style (V. Karoli)

Ingredients	6 portions	Method
Round steaks, ½ lb. each	6	Pound with rim of plate; season with salt and pepper.
Salt	to taste	
Pepper	to taste	
Flour	as needed	Dredge meat in flour; fry in large skillet until brown on both sides. Place steak in baking dish or pan.
Oil	⅓ cup	
Carrots, chopped	3	Add; bake at 375F for about 1 hour or until steaks are tender. Remove steaks from pan.
Onion, pared, chopped	1	
Celery rib, minced	½	
Tomato purée	2 cups	
Garlic cloves, pared, minced	2	
Sour cream	2 cups	Stir into sauce; reheat but do not boil. Serve steak with gravy on buttered noodles.

Beefsteak and Onions in Sour Cream (A. Wisnesky)

Ingredients	4 portions	Method
New York strip steak, cooked, julienne cut	1 lb.	Combine.
Medium red onion, pared, julienne	1	
Lemon juice	1 oz.	
Pepper	to taste	Season meat.
Salt	to taste	
Sour cream	1 cup	Blend in; mix well.
Chives, chopped	as needed	Serve on lettuce leaf. Sprinkle with chopped chives.
Lettuce	as needed	

Beef Medallion Helga

(K. Loos)

Ingredients	4 portions	Method
English muffins	4	Cut into 8 half pieces; toast crisp in butter.
Butter	as needed	
Canadian bacon slices, 1 oz. each	8 oz.	Sauté bacon in butter and wine; place on English muffin.
Butter	12 oz.	
Sherry	3 oz.	
Beef medallions, 3 oz. each	24 oz.	Sauté; place on bacon.
Shallots, pared, minced	2	
Salt	to taste	
Pepper	to taste	
Pineapple rings	8	Sauté; place on medallions.
Monterey Jack cheese slices, 1 oz. each	8	Top each medallion; place under broiler until cheese has melted.
Mushroom caps, sautéed in butter	8	Place 1 on each medallion; season to taste. Serve on plate with watercress.

First Place Best Beef Chili '82

(H. Meadows)

Ingredients	8 portions	Method
Sirloin steak, medium dice, fat trimmed	2 lb.	Sauté in butter over medium heat for 5 minutes.
Pork loin, medium dice, fat trimmed	1 lb.	
Butter	½ lb.	
Garlic cloves, pared, minced	3	Add; simmer for 10 minutes.
Onions, pared, medium dice	1½ cups	
Green bell pepper, medium dice	1½ cups	
Celery, medium dice	1½ cups	
Green chilies	1 cup	
Parsley, chopped	¼ cup	
Tomato juice	2 cups	Add; heat to simmering.
Tomato purée	2 cups	
Fresh tomatoes, pared, medium dice	2 cups	
Beer	1 cup	
Chili powder	4 Tbsp.	Add; simmer slowly for 2 hours.
Cumin	1 Tbsp.	
Worcestershire sauce	2 Tbsp.	
Sugar	2 Tbsp.	
Chicken base	1 Tbsp.	

Machaca Beef (F. Clary)

Ingredients	8-10 portions	Method
Beef chuck, 2-in. thick	1½ lb.	Cut into 4-6 equal pieces; place in saucepan.
Salt	1 Tbsp.	Add; cover with water. Simmer for 3-3½ hours.
Pepper	1 tsp.	Remove from heat and liquid. Let cool enough to
Garlic clove, pared, crushed	1	hand shred meat.
Lard	1 Tbsp.	Heat in skillet.
Onion, pared, medium dice	5 oz.	Add with shredded beef; sauté.
Fresh jalpeno pepper, minced	1	
Yellow bell pepper, minced	1	
Fresh coriander sprigs, chopped	10	
Medium tomatoes, medium dice	3	Add; mix thoroughly.
Cumin	1 Tbsp.	
Chili powder	1 Tbsp.	
Salt	to taste	Adjust seasonings. Serve in taco shell or as tostado
Pepper	1 tsp.	with shredded lettuce and shredded cheese.

French Pasties (S. Muthofer)

Ingredients	6 portions	Method
Ground beef, 85% lean	6 oz.	Add; glaze until onions are done.
Onion, pared, chopped	1 Tbsp.	
Green bell pepper, chopped	1½ tsp.	
Salt	¼ tsp.	
Pepper	pinch	
Taco seasoning	¾ tsp.	
Garlic powder	pinch	
Tomatoes, ¼-in. dice	½ cup	Add; drain mix and cool.
Longhorn cheese, shredded	1½ oz.	
Frozen puff pastry, 5x5-in. squares	6	Place 6 squares on sheet pan. Spoon 2 heaping Tbsp. mix on diagonal half of each square; brush outsides with eggwash. Fold dough to form triangle. Press ends together. Brush triangle with eggwash; bake at 375F for 20 minutes.
Eggwash	as needed	
Lettuce, shredded	6 oz.	Serve with pastries.
Longhorn cheese, shredded	6 oz.	
Tomatoes, small dice	9 oz.	
Parsley sprigs	6	
Prepared taco sauce	12 oz.	

100 MPH Chili
(K. Elmer)

Ingredients	4½ qt.	Method
Pork, lean, ½-in. cubes	2½ lb.	Dust meat with flour.
Beef, ½-in. cubes	2½ lb.	
Flour	4 oz.	
Oil	2 oz.	Brown meat in small batches in hot oil; place in heavy brazier.
Onions, pared, sliced	1 lb.	Sauté; add to meat.
Canned beef stock with tomatillas, drained, squeezed	1 No. 2½ can	Add; stir well. Heat to boiling; reduce to simmering, stirring occasionally for about 60 minutes until pork and beef are tender.
Green chilies, medium dice	1 No. 303 can	
Tomato paste	3 oz.	
Garlic powder	½ tsp.	
Cumin	1 tsp.	
Salt	1 tsp.	
Pepper	1 Tbsp.	
Chili powder	1 Tbsp.	
Cayenne pepper	1 Tbsp.	
Paprika	2 Tbsp.	
Canned tomatoes, diced in purée	1 No. 2½ can	Add; heat to boiling.
Masa harina	1 oz.	Add; stir well. Simmer for 15 minutes. Ladle 10 oz. into serving casseroles; top with 2 avocado wedges and Monterey Jack cheese; melt under salamander.

Slices of Filet Mignon Sautéed in Red Wine
(A. Schrott)

Ingredients	1 portion	Method
Filet mignon slices, 3 oz. each	2	Sauté; reserve.
Butter	1 Tbsp.	
Shallots, pared, chopped	½ tsp.	Add to same pan; cook for 2 minutes.
Mushroom tops, chopped	4	
Red wine	2 oz.	Add red wine; reduce by half. Finish with brown sauce. Pour over mignon.
Brown sauce	2 oz.	
Parsley, chopped	garnish	Sprinkle over.

Beef Tips A La Dutch
(R. Buttner)

Ingredients	6 portions	Method
Tenderloin tips	2½ lb.	Trim and cut into bite-size pieces. Sauté in butter in large skillet.
Butter	2 Tbsp.	
Green bell peppers, julienne	2	Add; simmer until vegetables are half done.
Onion, pared, medium dice	1	
Mushrooms, sliced	2 cups	
Tomatoes, medium dice	1 cup	Add; simmer and reduce until liquid is thick.
Red wine	1½ cups	
Worcestershire sauce	½ cup	
Ketchup	1½ cups	
Salt	to taste	
Pepper	to taste	

Veal Scallops   (E. Mooser)

Ingredients	6 portions	Method
Milk-fed veal loin, trimmed	2 lb.	Slice thin; pound lightly.
Butter, clarified	¼ cup	Melt in sauté pan.
Salt White pepper Flour	to taste to taste as needed	Season veal; flour lightly. Sauté in butter. Remove from pan.
Shallots, pared, chopped	½ cup	Sauté in same pan; lightly dust with flour.
White wine Lemons, juiced	½ cup 2	Add; reduce slightly.
Fresh Thompson seedless grapes, lightly blanched Heavy cream	1 cup 1 cup	Add; reduce until sauce lightly coats back of spoon. Add veal; heat quickly to boiling. Serve immediately.

Beef Stroganoff   (P. Schmitt)

Ingredients	5 portions	Method
Tenderloin tips	1 lb.	Slice in thin slices, 2-in. x 1-in.
White vinegar White wine	¼ cup ¼ cup	Reduce by boiling for several minutes.
Brown sauce Sour cream	2½ cups ⅓ cup	Add, stirring constantly to prevent sauce from curdling.
Butter	3 Tbsp.	Stir in. Sauté tips in a heavy skillet until lightly browned; drain off fat.
Mushrooms, sliced	4 oz.	Sauté; add to beef. Add sauce to beef and mushrooms; heat through but do not boil.
Salt Pepper	to taste to taste	Adjust seasoning. Keep warm until ready to serve in a double boiler.

LAMB

Ethnic influences show in chefs' lamb recipes: (from top down) Curried Lamb Madras,
Roast Rack of Lamb with Herbs and Garlic Bread Crumbs, and Kebab a la Anglaise.

In the culinary sense, lamb is known in two forms: the milkfed lamb, which has not been weaned and has not yet been put out to graze; and the yearling lamb, a young sheep that has not yet reached its full size.

Good lamb can be recognized by the width of its loins, which should be well-covered with flesh, and by the color of its fat, which should be white and abundant around the kidneys. Lamb is tender meat with a delicate flavor.

If requested, lamb carcassses can be yield graded. Yield grades No. 2 and No. 3 are the major cutability grades and both give a high-quality product with a minimum of excess fat. Lamb has little marbling in the lean tissue, unlike beef. Lamb is therefore cooked to medium (160F) today to ensure a more tender, juicy product.

Baby lambs are sold whole mainly around Easter, but can now be obtained any time of year. Their weight is around 10 to 12 pounds. Yearling lambs are divided into cuts. The best parts are the legs, the saddle and the racks. The shoulders, neck and breasts are principally used for stews, curries, chops and ragouts.

Lamb legs usually are roasted, either whole or boned and tied. Two legs together are called double legs. When the saddle is left on with the legs, it is called a baron. This cut often is desirable for buffet dinners. Lamb shoulders can be stuffed, roasted or cut up for stews or ragouts.

—*Hermann Rusch*

Roast Rack of Lamb with Herbs (J. Monnke)

Ingredients	4-6 portions	Method
Rack of lamb, chine bones removed	4 lb.	Remove fat from ends of chop bones by cutting down each rib bone about halfway toward base. Trim fat and score.
Salt	1 Tbsp.	Rub meat all over with salt.
Tarragon, minced	1½ tsp.	Combine; rub over all meat surfaces. Roast at 450F with fat side down for 15 minutes and fat side up for 10 minutes.
Chives, minced	1½ tsp.	
Shallots, pared, minced	1½ tsp.	
Parsley	1½ tsp.	
Bread crumbs	½ cup	Combine. Sprinkle over outside surfaces of lamb rack; return to oven for 5 minutes. Let stand for 10 minutes before slicing.
Fresh parsley, chopped	2 Tbsp.	
Garlic cloves, pared, minced	2	

Curried Lamb Madras (G. Grimeissen)

Ingredients	4 portions	Method
Frozen lamb shoulder, boneless	2 lb.	Trim all excess fat from meat; cut into 1-in. cubes.
Madras curry powder	3 Tbsp.	Season meat; rub into meat well.
Garlic clove, pared, minced	½	
Salt	to taste	
Pepper	to taste	
Paprika	½ tsp.	
Whole oregano, crushed	½ tsp.	
Ginger powder	¼ tsp.	
Flour	⅓ cup	Dust meat.
Margarine or butter	6 Tbsp.	Sauté; do not brown. Add meat, stirring frequently. Let smother in own moisture for several minutes.
Medium onion, pared, medium dice	½	
Medium apple, medium dice	½	
Fresh pineapple slice, medium dice	½	
Broth	2½ cups	Add; cover casserole. Let simmer until meat is tender. Adjust seasoning. Serve with boiled rice and mango chutney.

Kebab a la Anglaise   (K. Muller)

Ingredients	6 portions	Method
Lamb, boned leg meat	2 lb.	Cut into 32 1-oz. pieces. Place in bowl.
Fresh parsley, chopped	2 tsp.	Add to meat in bowl. Cover tightly; marinate for 1-2 days in refrigerator. Turn meat once or twice to even marination.
Fresh mint, chopped	2 Tbsp.	
Black peppercorns, crushed	½ tsp.	
Rosemary, crushed	½ tsp.	
Basil	½ tsp.	
Garlic clove, pared, minced with 1½ tsp. salt	½	
Dry white wine	¼ cup	
Oil	¼ cup	
Lemon juice	½ tsp.	
Green, red or yellow bell peppers	2	Cut in half lengthwise. Remove seeds; wash. Cut each half into 8 pieces.
Small onions	2	Cut in quarters, lengthwise from core down.
Firm cherry tomatoes	24	For each kebab, use 3 cherry tomatoes, 3 pieces of meat, peppers and onions in the following manner (1 each): cherry tomato, green pepper, onion, meat, pepper, onion, meat, cherry tomato, meat, green pepper.

Barbecued Lamb Chops Marinated in Spiced Vinegar   (S. Inonog)

Ingredients	4 portions	Method
Lamb chops	4 lb.	Trim excess fat.
Rice wine	1 cup	Mix together. Add lamb chops; marinate overnight. Barbecue in open charcoal pit. Cook to order. Baste with marinade while cooking. Serve in casserole dish garnished with scallion fan.
Palm vinegar	½ cup	
Garlic cloves, pared, crushed	2	
Peppercorns, crushed	1 tsp.	
Bay leaves	2	
Salt	to taste	

Medallions of Lamb Sauté Picatta   (R. Agostini)

Ingredients	4 portions	Method
Lamb loin portions, sliced in half, 6 oz. each	4	Flatten medallions between sheets of waxed paper to approximately ¼-in. thick.
Oil	½ cup	Place oil in sauté pan over moderate heat.
Flour	½ lb.	Combine; dredge lamb in mixture. Place lamb in pan; brown lightly on both sides for 2 minutes each. Remove lamb; place on desired serving plate.
Salt	to taste	
Black pepper, cracked	to taste	
Mushrooms, sliced, blanched	1 cup	Add to pan.
Fresh lemon juice	1 cup	
Chicken broth	1 cup	Add; let simmer until stock thickens slightly.
Fresh parsley, chopped	2 oz.	Add; pour sauce over lamb. Serve immediately with rice pilaf.

Marinated Rack of Spring Lamb

(F. Nikodemus)

Ingredients portions		Method
Vegetable oil	2 cups	Combine thoroughly; reserve.
Onion, pared, sliced	1	
Black peppercorns	1 Tbsp.	
Rosemary	to taste	
Racks of lamb, trimmed	2	Remove any meat or tissue from rib bones (rib bones should be cut down to 3 to 3½ inches). Marinate in reserved marinade in refrigerator for 48 hours. Remove from marinade; bake at 450F for about 30 minutes or until done.

Lamb Cushion with Tarragon

(H. Rusch)

Ingredients	6 portions	Method
Lamb loin fillets, 6 oz. each, trimmed, cut into 6-in.-long rectangles	6	Sprinkle lamb with seasonings.
Salt	to taste	
Pepper	to taste	
Butter, clarified	⅓ cup	Heat butter in a skillet; add garlic. Add lamb; sauté for 4 minutes on each side. Transfer to heated serving platter; reserve, covered, for 3 minutes before serving.
Garlic cloves, pared, crushed	2	
Shallots	2 Tbsp.	Add to skillet; sauté until golden. Drain butter.
Tarragon stems	6	
White wine	½ cup	Add; heat to boiling.
Brown sauce	½ cup	Add; simmer for 3 minutes. Strain; heat to boiling.
Vinegar	1 Tbsp.	Add; combine thoroughly. Serve over lamb.
Brandy	1 Tbsp.	
Butter, room temperature	1 Tbsp.	
Tarragon leaves, chopped	1 Tbsp.	

Marinated Broiled Lamb

(D. Jaramillo)

Ingredients	6-8 portions	Method
Medium onion, pared, diced	1	Combine thoroughly; pour into a large pan.
Olive or vegetable oil	½ cup	
Wine vinegar	½ cup	
Parsley, chopped	⅓ cup	
Salt	4 tsp.	
Rosemary, crushed	4 tsp.	
Thyme	1 Tbsp.	
Marjoram	1 Tbsp.	
Garlic cloves, pared, crushed	4	
Pepper	1 tsp.	
Lamb chops, 1½- to 2-in. thick, trimmed	16	Add; marinate in refrigerator overnight. Cook chops on gas or charcoal grill for 4 or 5 minutes on each side (do not overcook; lamb should be pink). Serve immediately with apple and mint jelly.

PORK

Academy chefs' pork recipes combine old-world flair with today's presentation: (clockwise from top) Grinzinger Heurigensalat, Dixie Pork Chops and Pork Fillet with Hazelnuts.

Pork was the most consumed meat until 1952 when beef surpassed it. Barrows (castrated males) and gilts (unbred females) provide the majority of the pork supply. As with older bulls, cows and dairy cattle, boars and sows are used in ground and processed products such as sausage when they are no longer useful as breeders. It is as wholesome as the younger product, but tougher.

Sows have a gestation period of three months, three weeks and three days. Hogs are marketed at about 6 months of age. The percentage of lean in today's pork is greater than it was in the past because of improved feeding.

Pork is eaten either fresh or cured. Its flesh lends itself readily to smoking, salting and making of all types of sausages. A ham is a leg of pork that has been salted and smoked. After boiling in plain water, ham can be baked or served cold. The parts of loins, fillet and leg (either ham or corned) are the choice morsels. The shoulder, head, bacon, spareribs and fatback also are fine products. —*Hermann Rusch*

Dixie Pork Chops (W. O'Neill)

Ingredients	8 portions	Method
Pork chops	8	Brown chops in hot shortening. Remove chops to baking dish; reserve fat.
Shortening	3 Tbsp.	
Salt	½ tsp.	Sprinkle over chops.
Sage	½ tsp.	
Apples, cored, cut into rings	4	Place apple rings on chops; sprinkle with sugar; reserve.
Brown sugar	¼ cup	
Flour	2 Tbsp.	Add to reserved fat; cook until thick.
Hot water	1 cup	
Vinegar	to taste	
Raisins	½ cup	Add; pour over chops. Bake, uncovered, at 350F for 1 hour.

Pork Fillet with Hazelnuts (W. Daffinger)

Ingredients	3 portions	Method
Pork tenderloin, trimmed	14 oz.	Slice pork into 6 portions; flatten to about ¼-inch thick. Sprinkle with salt and pepper.
Salt	to taste	
Pepper	to taste	
Flour	1 tsp.	Coat each portion in flour, then egg, then hazelnuts.
Egg, lightly beaten	1	
Hazelnuts, toasted, ground	4½ oz.	
Butter	2 Tbsp.	Place in heated pan; add pork medallions; brown on both sides. Remove from pan; reserve.
Shallot, pared, chopped	1	Add to pan; sauté until golden.
Flour	as needed	Sprinkle over shallot.
Heavy cream	¾ cup	Add; simmer for 3 minutes. Add reserved pork medallions.
White wine	¼ cup	
Hazelnuts, toasted, ground	1 Tbsp.	
Lemon, juice of	¼	Add; taste and adjust seasonings; simmer for 4 additional minutes. Serve hot with spinach noodles or risotto.
Worcestershire sauce	to taste	
Chicken stock	¾ cup	

Grinzinger Heurigensalat (F. Buck)

Ingredients	10 portions	Method
Vegetable oil	1 cup	Mix; stir well.
Vinegar	¾ cup, 2 Tbsp.	
Ketchup	3 Tbsp.	
Mustard	1 Tbsp., 2 tsp.	
Water	as needed	
Worcestershire sauce	to taste	
Salt	to taste	
Pepper	to taste	
Sugar	to taste	
Salad potatoes, boiled, cut into thin slices	1 lb., 1 oz.	Combine; add.
Tomatoes, cut into quarters	5	
Green bell peppers, julienne	3	
Boiled beef, cut into thin slices	10 oz.	
Cervelat sausage, cut into thin slices	10 oz.	
Cold roast pork, cut into thin slices	10 oz.	
Green beans, boiled, julienne	8 oz.	
Onion, pared, julienne	7 oz.	
Gherkins, julienne	5 oz.	
Lettuce leaves	as needed	Line each plate with lettuce leaves; top with salad. Garnish with eggs and chives.
Hard-cooked eggs, cut into 6 equal parts	5	
Chives, minced	2 oz.	

Sweet-Sour Pork with Vegetables (P. Schmitt)

Ingredients	4 portions	Method
Pork butt or shoulder, cut into 1-in. cubes	1 lb.	Combine well.
Shoyu	1 Tbsp.	
Garlic clove, pared, minced	½	
Gingerroot, pared, minced	to taste	
Egg yolk	1	Add; combine well.
Cornstarch	1 Tbsp.	
Vegetable oil	as needed	Deep fry until ¾ done; reserve.
Bamboo shoots	½ cup	Sauté over high heat for 2 minutes.
Shiitake mushrooms, fresh or dried	3	
Vegetable oil	1 Tbsp.	
Sugar	¾ cup	Add; boil for 4 minutes.
Soup stock	½ to ¾ cup	
Vinegar	½ cup	
Shoyu	3 Tbsp.	
Ketchup	3 Tbsp.	
Sake	1 Tbsp.	
Cornstarch	2 Tbsp.	Mix; add; cook until thick; remove from heat.
Water	2 Tbsp.	
Sesame seed oil	1 tsp.	
Green peas, cooked	1-2 Tbsp.	Sprinkle over pork just before serving.

Pork Fillet in Sour Cream (F. Metz)

Ingredients	6 portions	Method
Butter	1 tsp.	Heat in skillet.
Oil	1 tsp.	
Pork fillets, 8 oz. each, trimmed	6	Add; heat until brown.
Rosemary, chopped	½ tsp.	Add; roast at 375F for 15 to 20 minutes. Remove pork and bay leaf; reserve pan drippings in skillet. Slice fillets; place on skewers.
Bay leaf	½	
Salt	to taste	
Pepper	to taste	
Sour Cream Sauce	recipe follows	Serve over bed of noodles with reserved sauce and parsley.
Parsley, chopped	as needed	

Sour Cream Sauce (for Pork Fillet in Sour Cream) (F. Metz)

Ingredients	6 portions	Method
Onions, pared, chopped	1½	Sauté in reserved skillet until light brown.
Ham, julienne	¾ cup	
Mushrooms, julienne	¾ cup	
Butter	1 Tbsp.	
Garlic cloves, pared, chopped	2	
Pickles, julienne	½ cup	Add.
Dry white wine	1 cup	Deglaze; heat until reduced to 2 cups.
Brown sauce	1½ cups	Combine; add. Heat to boiling; remove from heat.
Prepared mustard	2 tsp.	
Sour cream	½ cup	Add; combine thoroughly (do not boil).
Salt	to taste	
Pepper	to taste	

Apritada Carne at Baboy (S. Inonog)

Ingredients	4 portions	Method
Bottom beef round, 1-in. dice	1 lb.	Brown beef in oil; remove beef; reserve.
Peanut oil	¼ cup	
Garlic clove, pared, crushed	1	Add to pan; sauté for 1 minute.
Medium onion, minced	1	
Tomato sauce	2 cups	
Pork butt, 1-in. dice	8 oz.	Add with reserved beef; sauté for another 2 minutes.
Large potato, cut into 1-x-2-in. sticks	1	Add; let simmer for 20 minutes.
Beef stock	1 qt.	
Medium red bell pepper, 1-in. dice	1	Add; simmer for 10 minutes.
Medium green bell pepper, 1-in. dice	1	
Stuffed green olives	1 cup	Add; simmer for 2 minutes. Serve with fried rice or plain boiled rice.
Salt	to taste	

PORK

Sweet and Pungent Pork
(R. Kinney)

Ingredients	1 portion	Method
Pork tenderloin medallions, 2 oz. each	3	Sprinkle seasonings over pork; dust with flour.
Salt	to taste	
Pepper	to taste	
Flour	as needed	
Butter	1 oz.	Sauté pork.
Green bell pepper, blanched, cut into diamonds	1 oz.	Add; sauté lightly.
Pineapple, fresh, cut into chunks	1 oz.	
Bamboo shoots, sliced	1 oz.	
Water chestnuts, sliced	1 oz.	
Sweet and sour sauce	3 oz.	Add; heat to boiling.
Watercress sprigs	as needed	Place pork in center of hot dinner plate; cover with vegetable sauce; garnish with watercress.

Roast Marinated Pork Loin
(G. Shaffer)

Ingredients	4-6 portions	Method
Pork loin, 3 to 5 lb.	1	Place in large bowl.
Dry white wine	1½ cups	Combine; add. Marinate pork, turning occasionally, in refrigerator for 3 or 4 days. Drain pork; reserve marinade. Dry pork with paper toweling; place on rack in baking pan. Roast, basting occasionally with reserved marinade, at 325F for 40 minutes for each pound. When done, turn off heat. Leave pork in oven for 10 minutes.
Carrot, pared, sliced	½ cup	
Onion, pared, sliced	½ cup	
Peppercorns	1 tsp.	
Thyme	1 tsp.	
Juniper berries	1 tsp.	
Garlic cloves, pared, crushed	3	
Large bay leaf	1	

Tomato and Green Pepper Ragout
(S. Rakoczy)

Ingredients	4-6 portions	Method
Lard or bacon fat	3 Tbsp.	Heat in a 2-qt. saucepan or casserole until light haze forms over it.
Onions, pared, minced	1½ cups	Add; cook for 8-10 minutes, until onions are golden.
Garlic clove, pared, minced	½ tsp.	
Sweet Hungarian paprika	2 Tbsp.	Add; stir until onions are well-coated.
Green bell peppers, seeded	1 lb.	Add; cover pan. Cook for 10 minutes over medium heat. (If tomatoes do not produce enough liquid to cover vegetables, add ¼ cup or more of purée.)
Tomatoes, seeded, peeled, coarsely chopped	1 lb.	
Pepper, freshly ground	½ tsp.	
Hungarian Debreceni sausage, cut into ⅛-in. slices	1 lb.	Add; cover. Simmer for 30 minutes.

Stuffed Pork Chops

(F. Sgro)

Ingredients	6 portions	Method
Celery, chopped	⅓ cup	Sauté until light brown.
Onion, pared, chopped	⅓ cup	
Butter or margarine	¼ cup	
Sausage meat	⅓ cup	Add; cook for 10 minutes; let cool.
White bread slices, 2 or 3 days old, soaked in milk, squeezed dry	6	Combine; add.
Apples, pared, diced	¾ cup	
Parsley, chopped	2 Tbsp.	
Egg	1	
Salt	to taste	
Pepper	to taste	
Pork chops, center cut, 6 oz. each, with pockets for stuffing	6	Stuff sausage mixture into pork chops.
Flour	¼ cup	Dust chops.
Vegetable oil	as needed	Heat chops in oil until brown; remove to baking dish.
Brown gravy, thin	as needed	Cover with; bake at 350F for 1½ hours.

Sauerkraut Balls

(C. Angelo)

Ingredients	10-12 portions	Method
Ham, cooked	8 oz.	Combine; grind, using medium or fine knife.
Pork, cooked	8 oz.	
Corned beef, cooked	8 oz.	
Medium onion, pared, minced	1	Add; sauté until brown.
Parsley, chopped	to taste	
Flour	2 cups	Combine; sift once; add.
Dry mustard	1 tsp.	
Salt	1 tsp.	
Milk	2 cups	Add; cook until light and fluffy; let cool.
Sauerkraut	2 lb.	Add; grind; combine thoroughly. Roll into balls about the size of walnuts.
Flour	as needed	Coat each ball with flour, then egg, then bread crumbs. Deep fry; serve hot.
Egg, lightly beaten	as needed	
Bread crumbs	as needed	

PORK

Chinese Barbecued Pork   (E. Leong)

Ingredients	4 portions	Method
Soy sauce	½ cup	Combine in large mixing bowl.
Honey	⅓ cup	
Sherry	¼ cup	
Red food coloring	½ tsp.	
Gingerroot, pared, ground	¼ tsp.	
Garlic powder	¼ tsp.	
Boneless pork loin roast	2 lb.	Unroll pork roast; cut lengthwise into 3 strips. Add; turn several times to coat thoroughly. Marinate, covered, turning occasionally, in the refrigerator for 12 hours. Remove pork from sauce; reserve sauce. Place meat on rack in water bath; insert meat thermometer in thickest part of 1 strip. Roast at 325F for 30 minutes; turn meat; roast for 30 minutes or until meat thermometer registers 185F. Let cool slightly before slicing.
Sesame seeds, toasted	⅓ cup	Cut each strip into thin slices. Serve with reserved sauce, sesame seeds and mustard-soy sauce.
Mustard-soy sauce	as needed	

Pork Chops A La Schrott   (A. Schrott)

Ingredients	4 portions	Method
Medium potatoes, pared, cut into ¼-in. slices	8	Place in roasting pan.
Medium onion, pared, minced	1	Sprinkle over; reserve.
Caraway seeds	to taste	
Pork chops, ½-in. thick	8	Sauté in heavy skillet until brown.
Shortening	as needed	
Salt	to taste	Add; drain fat.
Pepper	to taste	
Beef broth	12 oz.	Deglaze; pour over reserved potatoes. Bake, uncovered, at 375F for 35 to 45 minutes.

Pork Tenderloin a la Française   (E. Foulard)

Ingredients	2 portions	Method
Pork tenderloin, trimmed	1 lb.	Rub tenderloin with salt and pepper.
Salt	as needed	
White pepper	as needed	
Bacon, long slice	1	Wrap tenderloin with bacon slice; roll in 1 or 2 layers cabbage. Arrange in narrow buttered baking pan or casserole with bay leaf underneath.
Green cabbage leaves, pre-blanched	as needed	
Bay leaf	1	
White wine	1 cup	Add wine; bake at 375F for 30 minutes or until pork is tender. As wine reduces, replace it with brown sauce. Remove pork to platter or casserole; slice. Adjust seasoning of sauce.
Brown sauce	¾ cup	
Sweet butter	1 Tbsp.	Lightly coat pork slices; serve the rest of sauce on the side.

NOTES

GAME

Exotic game, from venison to quail, are finding new prominence on menus: Venison
Chasseur with Chestnut Purée (top) and Roasted Quail in Champagne (bottom).

The term game applies to all wild animals and birds that are hunted and eaten. When applied to fish it means simply those fish that usually are large, such as barracuda, and are sometimes of coarse texture.

Game can be divided into four categories:

–Small birds—none larger than the quail or the thrush.

–Game proper—winged game (pheasant, partridge) and land game (wild rabbit, possum).

–Large game—such as deer, wild boar and moose.

–Game fish—such as barracuda.

Game is a healthful, savory food that is more strongly flavored than the meat of domesticated animals and birds but often is lower in fat and cholesterol. In the hands of an experienced cook, however, it need not be gamey tasting.

Wild game has a variety of flavors that are similar to what consumers are accustomed to: buffalo is the closest tasting meat to beef, pheasant resembles chicken and rattlesnake is a bland meat that is good with spicy sauces. All game meats should be bought from a licensed distributor to assure that it has been processed properly and that it conforms to the wildlife regulations.

—*John W. Kaufmann*

Venison Chasseur with Chestnut Purée (J. Deluhery)

Ingredients	10 portions	Method
Medium carrots, pared, chopped	2	Sauté.
Medium onions, pared, chopped	2	
Garlic cloves, pared, chopped	2	
Shallots, pared, chopped	2	
Celery ribs, chopped	2	
Olive oil	½ cup	
Rosemary	pinch	Add to sautéed vegetables. Simmer for 15 minutes; allow to cool.
Chervil	pinch	
Bay leaf	1	
Cloves	2	
Vinegar	1 cup	
White wine	1 qt.	
Water	1 qt.	
Medium tomatoes, medium dice	8	
Currant jelly	½ cup	
Venison loin or leg	12 lb.	Season lightly. Pour marinade over. Refrigerate for 36 hours; turn meat twice a day. Remove from marinade; drain. Roast at 375F for 45 minutes.
Salt	to taste	
Roux	as needed	Thicken marinade with roux to desired consistency. Add to venison; simmer for 15 minutes.
Chestnut purée	2 cups	Serve with venison.

Pressed Wild Duck (R. Bryan)

Ingredients	3 servings	Method
Young wild ducks, singed	3	Clean ducks; hang for 2 days. Rub inside and out with lemon juice, salt and pepper. Roast at 425F for 17 minutes. Carve off breasts; place in chafing dish. Place carcasses in well of duck press.
Salt	to taste	
Pepper	to taste	
Lemon juice	as needed	
Red wine, warmed	1 cup	Mix; put into press. Force sauce, blood and juice through press. Run through press three times. Pour sauce over breasts in chafing dish. Heat well but do not boil; serve with wild rice.
Sweet butter, melted	6 Tbsp.	
Goose liver pâté	¼ cup	
Cognac	2 Tbsp.	
Lemons, juiced	2	
Celery salt	⅔ tsp.	
Cayenne pepper	⅓ tsp.	

Roasted Quail in Champagne (E. Laqua)

Ingredients	4 portions	Method
Quails, boned Salt Pepper	8 to taste to taste	Season lightly.
Goose liver pâté Wild rice, cooked	1 oz. 1 cup	Stuff each quail.
Bacon slices	2	Place over quail; secure with wooden picks. Place in sauté pan; roast at 400F for 15-20 minutes. Discard grease, leaving drippings in pan.
Dry champagne Au jus Demi-glace	2 oz. 1 oz. 1 oz.	Add to pan; reduce by a third.
Duchesse potato mix	as needed	Pipe two nests of prepared duchesse potatoes on plate. Place quails in nests. Pour sauce over quails.
White grapes, heated	garnish	Garnish with heated grapes.

Venison Stew In Red Wine (H. Rusch)

Ingredients	6 portions	Method
Venison shoulder, neck and top of the loin	6 lb.	Cut into 1¼-in. dice; place in a crock.
Red wine Oil Thyme Rosemary	2 cups 2 cups 2 tsp. 1 tsp.	Mix; pour over meat to cover. Marinate 2-3 days. Remove meat from marinade; drain and pat dry.
Salt Pepper	to taste to taste	Season.
Flour Butter, clarified	½ cup ½ cup	Dredge meat in flour; brown in butter in a sauté pan until light brown. Put meat into casserole; sprinkle with the rest of the flour. Set casserole in 400F oven for 5 minutes.
Brown stock	1 cup	Add with 1 cup marinade meat. Cover; cook at 325F for 1½ hours.
Salt pork pieces, ¾-in. dice	24	Heat in sauté pan; let render part of fat.
Mushrooms, cut into quarters Pearl onions, blanched	8 24	Add to pork cubes; sauté for 3 minutes. When stew is done, separate meat; place in saucepan. Strain sauce onto meat.
Brandy	3 Tbsp.	Add with pork-cube mixture; heat to boiling. Let simmer for ½ hour.
Salt Pepper	to taste to taste	Adjust seasoning; place in serving bowls.
Bread croutons, heart-shaped, sautéed	12	Garnish; complement with spaetzle noodles.

Hasenpfeffer (P. Ambros)

Ingredients	4 portions	Method
Rabbit, about 2 lb., cut into 2 pieces (2 legs and saddle)	1	Rinse meat; pat dry with paper toweling. Rub with salt.
Salt	1½ tsp.	
Butter or margarine	3 Tbsp.	Sauté meat for about 30 minutes or until brown. Remove to casserole.
Medium onion, pared	1	Stud onion with cloves; add.
Cloves	4	
Stock or bouillon, hot	3 cups	Add; bake, covered, at 350F for 2½ to 3 hours.
Port or claret	¾ cup	
Lemon juice	1 Tbsp.	
Peppercorns	12	
Bouquet garni	1	
Butter	1 Tbsp.	About ½ hour before serving, heat butter until melted. Add flour; stir into rabbit mixture.
Flour	1 Tbsp.	
Port or claret	¾ cup	Add; taste and adjust seasonings. Bake, covered, at 350F for 30 minutes. Arrange meat on serving dish; strain gravy over. Serve with red currant jelly.

Cranberry-stuffed Pheasant (P. Ambros)

Ingredients	4 portions	Method
Pheasants, 3 lb. each	2	Rinse pheasants; pat dry with paper toweling. Rub inside and outside with lemon; sprinkle with seasonings.
Lemon, cut in half	1	
Salt	to taste	
Paprika	to taste	
Cranberries, fresh	1½ cups	Combine in saucepan; simmer for about 10 minutes or until cranberries are tender.
Sugar	1 cup	
Water	¾ cup	
Dry white wine or white-wine vinegar, diluted	½ cup	Drain cranberries; reserve. Add wine to cranberry syrup; reserve.
Butter or margarine	½ cup	Heat butter until melted; sauté until golden.
Onion, pared, diced	1	
Small apples, pared, cored, chopped	2	Stir in with reserved drained cranberries. Stuff pheasants with apple mixture; sew or skewer openings. Truss pheasants; place on rack in shallow baking pan.
Bacon strips	6	Place bacon over breasts. Roast, basting every 15 minutes with reserved syrup, at 350F for 1½ hours or until tender. Arrange pheasants on heated platter. Skim fat from pan drippings; serve pheasant and stuffing with pan drippings and wild rice.

Brandied Duck (P. Lenard)

Ingredients	4 portions	Method
Mallard ducks, cut into pieces	2	Rinse ducks; sprinkle with seasonings.
Salt	to taste	
Pepper	to taste	
Large onions, pared, chopped	2	Combine; add. Marinate for 4 hours.
Claret	2 cups	
Brandy	3 oz.	
Parsley, chopped	1 tsp.	
Thyme	¼ tsp.	
Bay leaf	1	
Garlic clove, pared, crushed	1	
Olive oil	¼ cup	Pour oil into casserole. Remove ducks from marinade; reserve marinade. Heat ducks in casserole until brown.
Mushrooms	½ lb.	Add with reserved marinade. Cook, covered, over low heat until duck is tender.

Venison Stew with Dumplings (P. Ambros)

Ingredients	4 portions	Method
Venison neck or shoulder meat or shoulder chops	3 lb.	Trim all fat, cartilage and sinew; cut meat into 1½-in. pieces.
Flour	⅓ cup	Combine; dredge meat in flour mixture.
Salt	1½ tsp.	
Paprika	1 tsp.	
Pepper	¼ tsp.	
Bacon drippings or shortening	¼ cup	Heat bacon or shortening in large, deep saucepan until melted. Add meat; heat until brown on all sides.
Water	3½ cups	Add; combine thoroughly. Simmer, covered, for 2 hours or until meat is tender. Refrigerate overnight or for at least several hours. Carefully remove all solidified fat; blot edges of pan with paper toweling. Remove and discard marrow bones, bay leaf, parsley and celery.
Medium onion, pared, sliced	1	
Celery ribs with leaves	2	
Marrow bones	as needed	
Parsley sprigs	4	
Bay leaf	1	
Small white onions, pared	12	Add; cook until heated through. Reserve warm.
Medium carrots, pared, cut in half	6	
Medium potatoes, pared, cut in half	3	
Worcestershire sauce	2 tsp.	
Flour, sifted	3 cups	Sift together.
Baking powder	3 tsp.	
Salt	1 tsp.	
Shortening	2 Tbsp.	Cut in until mixture resembles coarse crumbs.
Milk	1 cup	Add; stir in until just combined. Drop dough by spoonfuls onto pieces of meat or vegetables. Simmer, uncovered, for 10 minutes. Cook, tightly covered, until vegetables are done.

Venison Ragout   (B. Urban)

Ingredients	10 portions	Method
Mirepoix (diced, pared carrots, onions and celery)	1 lb.	Combine thoroughly.
Burgundy	2 qt.	
Wine vinegar	1 cup	
Juniper berries	1 tsp.	
Peppercorns	8	
Bay leaves	2	
Cloves	3	
Venison breast, boned, cut into ½-in. cubes	4 lb.	Add; combine thoroughly. Marinate meat in refrigerator, stirring occasionally, for 1 week.
Vegetable oil, hot	½ cup	Drain meat; reserve marinade liquid; separate meat and mirepoix. Quickly heat meat in hot oil until brown. Add mirepoix; sauté.
Flour	6 oz.	Sprinkle over; sauté until brown. Add reserved marinade liquid; heat to boiling.
Beef stock	1 qt.	Strain; pour stock with marinade over meat. Taste and adjust seasonings. Simmer until meat is tender. Remove meat; strain sauce; pour sauce over meat.
Salt	1 tsp.	
Bacon slices, sautéed	6 oz.	Arrange bacon and mushrooms over top of ragout. Serve with noodles, spaetzle or whipped potatoes.
Mushrooms, fresh, sliced, sautéed	12 oz.	

Breast of Pheasant Under Glass   (H. Rusch)

Ingredients	2 portions	Method
Pheasant breasts (from 3-lb. pheasant)	2	Remove skin; leave wing bone extending 1 in. from breast. Trim edges; lightly flatten with side of knife.
Lemon, juice of	½	Rub with lemon juice; sprinkle with seasonings.
Salt	to taste	
Pepper	to taste	
Butter	2 Tbsp.	Poach breasts in foaming butter for about 3 minutes on each side (do not overcook; juice should be clear yellow and meat pink). Place each breast in a round gratin dish; reserve.
Shallots	1 tsp.	Add shallots to same skillet; sauté until golden.
Brandy	2 Tbsp.	Drain butter; pour in brandy; add wine. Heat to boiling; cook until reduced by half.
White wine	⅓ cup	
Heavy cream	½ cup	Add; heat until reduced to coating consistency.
Meat glaze	1 Tbsp.	
Lemon, juice of	½	Strain sauce into bowl; add.
Butter	1 Tbsp.	
Cayenne pepper	to taste	
Truffles, julienne	1 Tbsp.	Portion truffles and mushrooms over reserved breasts. Ladle sauce over. Cover with glass bell, buttered inside, fitting exactly in gratin dish. Heat sauce to boiling; simmer for 2 minutes. Serve immediately.
Mushrooms, cooked, julienne	2 Tbsp.	

'Mute' Duck with Pepper Sauce (L. Zara)

Ingredients	4 portions	Method
Cabernet sauvignon	375 ml.	Combine.
Medium onion, pared, chopped	1	
Medium carrot, pared, chopped	1	
Celery rib, chopped	½	
Lemon, juice of	1	
Bouquet garni (rosemary, sage and bay leaf)	1	
Garlic clove, pared, crushed	1	
'Mute' duck or Long Island duck	1	Rinse duck; place in marinade. Marinade, turning occasionally, in refrigerator for 2 days. Remove duck from marinade; drain marinade; stuff duck with marinade vegetables.
Salt	to taste	Sprinkle duck with seasonings. Place in pan with oil and butter. Roast at 350F, basting occasionally, for 1 hour or until done.
Black pepper, freshly ground	to taste	
Vegetable oil	½ cup	
Butter	2 Tbsp.	
Pepper Sauce	recipe follows	Serve with.

Pepper Sauce
(for 'Mute' Duck with Pepper Sauce) (L. Zara)

Ingredients	4 portions	Method
Onion, pared, minced	1	Sauté until brown.
Butter	as needed	
Mortadella	5½ oz.	Grind together; add. Combine thoroughly.
Italian salami	4 oz.	
Liver	from duck	
Chicken liver	2 oz.	
Capers	2 oz.	
Anchovy fillets	6	
Cabernet sauvignon	4 oz.	Add; combine thoroughly. Reduce heat; simmer for 1½ hours.
Lemons, juice of	2	
Salt	to taste	
Pepper, freshly ground	to taste	
Bread crumbs	¼ cup	Stir in to thicken. Taste and adjust seasonings. Serve with 'Mute' duck.
Vinegar	to taste	

Old-fashioned Mincemeat (A. Davis)

Ingredients	12 portions	Method
Venison necks, flanks and less desirable cuts	2 lb.	Cook until meat is tender; remove from bones; grind coarsely.
Tart green apples, pared, cored, chopped	4 qt.	Combine; add; combine thoroughly. Cook until apples are soft.
Raisins, seedless	1 lb.	
Currants	½ lb.	
Quince, pared, cored, chopped	2 cups	
Citron, chopped	1 cup	
Brown sugar	1 cup	
Molasses, dark	½ cup	
Sherry	2 Tbsp.	
Rosewater	1 Tbsp.	
Lemon juice	1 Tbsp.	
Salt	2 Tbsp.	
Cinnamon	1 Tbsp.	
Mace	½ tsp.	
Cloves, ground	½ tsp.	
Brandy	½ cup	Add; cook for 1 minute. Remove from heat; let cool.

Pintade Au Fromage Persilee, Sauce Mandarin (L. Schaeli)

Ingredients	6 portions	Method
Petit Swiss or cream cheese	12 oz.	Combine thoroughly.
Mushrooms, minced	6 oz.	
Shallots, minced	6 oz.	
Parsley, chopped	½ cup	
Chives or scallions, chopped	¼ cup	
Tarragon, dried	3 tsp.	
Garlic cloves, pared, crushed	3	
Salt	to taste	
Pepper, freshly ground	to taste	
Guinea hens, 2 lb. each, backbones removed	3	Stuff guinea hens with cheese mixture. Brush with butter; roast, basting frequently, at 425F for about 30 minutes. Remove; reserve warm.
Butter, melted	6 oz.	
Chicken stock	2 cups	Add; deglaze. Cook until reduced by half.
White wine	4 oz.	
Orange-flavored liqueur	4 oz	
Mandarin wedges, seeded	6 oz	Serve reserved guinea hens with orange sauce and mandarin wedges.

Rabbit in Spiced Red Wine Sauce   (W. Kraemer)

Ingredients	4 portions	Method
Red wine vinegar	4 oz.	Mix.
Garlic cloves, pared	2	
Bay leaves	2	
Cloves	2	
Coarsely ground pepper	1 tsp.	
Thyme	1 tsp.	
Red table wine	750 mL.	
Rabbit, cut in 8 pieces	1	Marinate for 2 hours.
Fresh unsmoked pork belly, medium dice	1 lb.	Sauté until light brown. Drain marinade; reserve.
Flour	as needed	Dust rabbit pieces; brown in butter.
Butter	3 oz.	
Flour	4 Tbsp.	Place in roasting pan with reserved marinade; heat to boiling on range top, stirring frequently. Add rabbit, pork belly and diced onion mixture.
Rye bread, crumbled	10 oz.	Add. If sauce is too thick, dilute with a little water. Cover tightly; place in oven at 325F for 2 hours. Serve with homemade noodles.
Spice cake, crumbled	4-x-4-in. square	

Quail Pie, Rolling Rock   (W. Daffinger)

Ingredients	8 portions	Method
Quails, cut in half	8	Sprinkle quails with seasonings; dredge in flour.
Salt	to taste	
Pepper	to taste	
Flour	as needed	
Vegetable oil	as needed	Sauté until brown on both sides; remove; reserve.
Mushrooms, fresh	1 lb.	Add; sauté for 5 minutes.
Eschallots, cleaned	1 pt.	
Small onion, pared, diced	1	
Garlic cloves, pared, crushed	2	
Cognac	1½ oz.	Add with reserved quails; ignite.
Carrots	1 No. 303 can	Add; simmer for 5 minutes. Place quail and vegetables in casserole; reserve.
Peas	1 No. 303 can	
Salsify, broken	1 No. 303 can	
Parisienne potatoes, blanched	1½ cups	
Chicken broth	1 cup	
Port	½ cup	
Bay leaves	2	
Cloves	2	
Water	3½ Tbsp.	Combine water and flour to form paste; stir into same skillet; cook until thick. Taste and adjust seasonings; pour over reserved quail and vegetables.
Flour	2 Tbsp.	
Salt	to taste	
Pepper	to taste	
Prepared pie shell or puff pastry	as needed	Place pie shell over casserole; seal; cut vents to allow steam to escape. Bake at 350F until crust is brown.

Rabbit Stew

(M. Agius)

Ingredients	4 portions	Method
Medium rabbit, about 2 lb., disjointed	1	Heat in skillet until golden; reserve.
Olive oil	2 Tbsp.	Sauté in deep saucepan until translucent.
Onions, pared, diced	3	
Garlic cloves, pared, crushed	4	
Chicken stock	2 cups	Stir in; heat to slowly boiling.
Tomato paste	8 oz.	
Small new potatoes, pared	8	Add with reserved meat. Cook, covered, for about 20 minutes.
Burgundy	½ cup	
Bay leaves	2	
Peas, fresh or frozen	8 oz.	Add; taste and adjust seasonings. Cook for 5 minutes.
Salt	to taste	
Pepper	to taste	

Squirrel in Wine

(P. Lenard)

Ingredients	4 portions	Method
Squirrels, cut into pieces	4	Sauté until light brown.
Olive oil	¼ cup	
Butter	2 Tbsp.	
Dry white wine	1 cup	Add; simmer, turning meat often, until almost done.
Chicken broth	1 cup	
Rosemary	½ tsp.	
Garlic cloves, pared, crushed	2	
Salt	to taste	
Pepper	to taste	
Mushrooms, sliced	2 cups	Add; cook for 5 minutes.
Parsley, chopped	1 Tbsp.	

Roast Rock Cornish Hen 'Youghiogheny' with Wild Rice

(F. Ambrose)

Ingredients	4 portions	Method
Rock Cornish game hens, 16 oz. each	4	Brush hens with shortening; sprinkle with seasonings. Bake at 350F for about 25 minutes.
Shortening	½ cup	
Salt	to taste	
Pepper	to taste	
Onion, pared, minced	2 Tbsp.	Sprinkle over; bake for 30 minutes or until done. Remove hens; reserve warm.
Water	1 cup	Combine; add to pan drippings. Cook gently for about 5 minutes until flour is thoroughly combined.
Sherry	½ cup	
Flour	1 Tbsp.	
Sour cream	3 Tbsp.	Add; stir well. Place each reserved hen on heated serving plate; cover with gravy; serve with wild rice.
Chives, fresh, minced	1 tsp.	

PASTAS

The Italians are not the only ones with a passion for pasta, as academy chefs prove: (top to bottom) Lasagna Rolls, and Pesto and Angel Hair.

Incredible amounts of pasta of all shapes and textures are being consumed both at home and in the trendy ethnic restaurants throughout the United States. Each chef is vying to outdo his competitors in creating the ultimate pasta concoction using ingredients such as caviar and sweet roasted garlic cloves in ginger.

Domestic- and foreign-made pasta machines are flooding the market, attempting to sate the appetites of the American public. The true pasta aficionado continues to make fresh pasta by hand, using either a rolling pin or a hand roller and cutter in the belief that this is the only method of producing the very thin, fluffy pasta that is served in virtually every restaurant in Italy. The hand method allows the dough to rest between kneading and rolling, allowing one to feel the softness and know that the dough has rested without becoming elastic as it does when the dough is overworked.

There are approximately 135 types or shapes of pasta on the pasta market today. One was designed by a famous auto designer. Its shape is a racy design made to retain the sauce. The hardness of the Italian pasta is obtained from the finest durum wheat semolinas using only the heart of the kernels.

The best way to cook pasta is in the largest pot available to avoid starch buildup. Heat the water to a full boil, add salt to taste. Then add the pasta to the water, leaving the cover off. Start lifting strands with a two-tine long fork, separating the strands as the pasta is lifted and stirred. Reduce the heat to a slow boil until the pasta is very firm to the bite. Immediately drain, but do not rinse, and place a heaping tablespoon of butter in the pot used for cooking the pasta. Add the pasta to the pan and toss in the butter. **—Daniel Palmerone**

Pesto and Angel Hair (E. Newman)

Ingredients	10 portions	Method
Fresh basil	3 cups	Purée in food processor. Pour into small bowl.
Olive oil	¾ cup	
Pine nuts	¼ cup	
Garlic cloves, pared	3	
Salt	1 tsp.	
Parmesan cheese, freshly grated	½ cup	Add; mix until just blended. Adjust seasonings. Reserve.
Romano cheese, freshly grated	3 Tbsp.	
Water	1 gal.	Mix; heat to a rapid boil.
Salt	¼ tsp.	
Vegetable oil	½ oz.	
Angel-hair pasta	2 lb.	Add; cook 2-3 minutes; drain.
Butter	2 oz.	Heat in skillet. Add angel hair and ¾ cup reserved sauce.
White wine	½ oz.	Add; mix. Add remaining sauce; serve immediately.

Rice Risotto (S. Rakoczy)

Ingredients	6 portions	Method
Olive oil	⅔ cup	Heat in heavy skillet.
Scallions or leeks, chopped	1 cup	Add; sauté 3 minutes.
Mushrooms, chopped	1 cup	
Converted rice, uncooked	2 cups	Add; sauté 4 minutes.
Chicken stock	1 qt.	Add; bring to boil.
Peas	10 oz.	Add. Bake at 400F until liquid is absorbed in rice, 20-25 minutes.
Ham, smoked, chopped	1 cup	
Oregano	1 Tbsp.	
Rosemary	1 Tbsp.	

Lasagna Rolls (R. Soeder)

Ingredients	4 portions	Method
Lasagna	1 lb.	Prepare according to package directions. Rinse with cold water; drain on paper towels.
Ground beef	8 oz.	Brown in skillet; drain. Reserve meat at room temperature.
Spinach, rinsed, stems removed, chopped	½ cup	Cook in boiling water; drain well.
Ricotta cheese Italian cheese, grated	8 oz. ½ cup	Add to meat with cooked spinach.
Eggs, beaten	2	Add. Place lasagna on a flat surface; spread entire strip with meat mixture; roll slowly from end to end.
Tomato sauce Mozzarella cheese	2 cups ½ cup	Spoon 1 cup of the tomato sauce in bottom of baking pan; add lasagna rolls; top with remaining sauce and mozzarella. Bake at 350F about 30 minutes. Serve hot.

Spaetzle (A. Marty)

Ingredients	10 portions	Method
Flour Water Milk Farina, uncooked Eggs, beaten Egg yolks Nutmeg Salt Pepper	3 cups ½ cup ½ cup ½ cup 3 2 to taste to taste to taste	Mix well in a large bowl. Beat by hand until smooth but firm. Let rest 10 minutes.
Water	as needed	Bring to a boil. Press dough through a sieve with ½-in. holes into the boiling water. Return to a boil; remove spaetzle. Place in iced water. Drain well.
Butter, melted	½ cup	Sauté spaetzle in butter until golden.

Fettuccine al Burro (J. Piskor)

Ingredients	12 portions	Method
Butter	8 oz.	Beat until light and fluffy.
Heavy cream	½ cup	Add gradually; beating constantly until all cream is added.
Parmesan cheese, grated	1 cup	Add; mix until blended; cover; reserve.
Water Salt	3 qt. 3 Tbsp.	Bring water to a boil; add salt.
Fettuccine	2 lb.	Add; stir gently. Cook until tender for 5-8 minutes; drain well. Transfer to heated bowl. Add reserved butter mixture; toss until fettuccine is well-coated; serve.

Manicotti (A. Pefanis)

Ingredients	6 portions	Method
Vegetable oil	2 oz.	Sauté.
Large onion, pared, chopped	1	
Garlic cloves, pared, crushed	2	
Tomato purée	4 cups	Add; simmer for 1 hour; reserve.
Water	1 cup	
Parsley, chopped	2 Tbsp.	
Salt	1 Tbsp.	
Sugar	1 Tbsp.	
Oregano	1 tsp.	
Basil	1 tsp.	
Pepper	½ tsp.	
Flour	1½ cups	Combine; pour into a skillet until spread to 7- to 8-in. circle. Cook until beads form. Stack each crêpe on waxed paper; reserve.
Water	1½ cups	
Eggs	6	
Salt	¼ tsp.	
Ricotta cheese	2 lb.	Combine thoroughly. Spoon about ¼ cup of the filling onto uncooked side of reserved crêpe; roll up. Spoon reserved sauce into bottom of 10x12-in. baking pan. Place each crêpe seam side down in pan. Cover with remaining sauce.
Mozzarella cheese, grated	8 oz.	
Parmesan cheese	4 oz.	
Eggs	2	
Parsley, chopped	1 Tbsp.	
Salt	1 tsp.	
Pepper	¼ tsp.	
Mozzarella cheese	as needed	Sprinkle over. Bake at 325F for 30 minutes.
Parmesan cheese	as needed	

Spaghetti with Chicken Liver Sauce (A. Schrott)

Ingredients	5 portions	Method
Chicken livers, cleaned, blanched, drained	2 lb.	Sauté until golden; drain fat; reserve livers.
Butter	4 oz.	
Vegetable oil	2 oz.	Sauté slowly in heavy skillet.
Onion, pared, chopped	4 oz.	
Garlic clove, pared, crushed	1	Add.
Bay leaf, crushed	1	
Thyme, crushed	to taste	
Mushrooms, chopped	6 oz.	Add; let simmer slowly for 10 minutes.
Thin brown sauce	1 qt.	Add; boil for 30 minutes; skim.
Tomatoes, quartered	1 lb.	Add with browned chicken livers. Bring to boil; season to taste.
Spaghetti, cooked	1 lb.	Serve sauce over spaghetti; sprinkle with cheese.
Parmesan cheese, grated	5 oz.	

Macaroni and Cheese Supreme (M. Minor)

Ingredients	4-5 portions	Method
Elbow macaroni; uncooked	1½ cups	Cook according to package directions in boiling salted water until tender; drain well; reserve.
White bread slices, torn into small pieces Butter, melted	2 2 Tbsp.	Combine; toss lightly; reserve.
Water, lukewarm Milk Prepared chicken sauce base Dry mustard Salt	1½ cups 1½ cups 1 2⅝-oz. jar ½ tsp. ½ tsp.	Heat in heavy saucepan, whisking constantly with wire whisk, over medium heat to boiling. Boil, stirring, for 1 minute; remove from heat.
Sharp cheddar cheese, shredded	2 cups	Stir in until melted. Add reserved macaroni; combine thoroughly. Pour into buttered 1½-qt. casserole. Sprinkle reserved bread crumbs over. Bake at 350F for 25 to 35 minutes until heated through and bread crumbs are golden.

Chicken Fried Rice (R. Ebert)

Ingredients	4 portions	Method
Vegetable oil Onion, pared, diced Green bell pepper, diced	1 Tbsp., 1 tsp. 1 Tbsp., 1 tsp. 1 Tbsp., 1 tsp.	Sauté until slightly tender.
Rice, cooked, chilled Chicken, cooked, diced	1 qt. 1 cup	Add; heat thoroughly.
Soy sauce Black pepper Salt	1 Tbsp. ¼ tsp. ¼ tsp.	Add; mix thoroughly until rice turns brown.
Eggs Vegetable oil	3 as needed	Beat eggs lightly; scramble in hot oil, beating constantly until light and fluffy; add; mix well; serve hot.

Spaghetti Roger (R. Cortello)

Ingredients	8 portions	Method
Tomatoes, medium, peeled, cut in half, seeded, chopped Anchovy fillets, chopped Garlic cloves, pared, chopped Black pepper Rosemary Whole thyme Olive oil, warmed	5 3 oz. 3 ½ tsp. to taste 1 sprig as needed	Mix in a gallon saucepan; cook slowly for 10 minutes.
Tomato purée Tomato paste	3 cups 6 oz.	Add just before serving; cook for 5-10 minutes.
Spaghetti	2 lb.	Cook according to package directions. Drain; rinse with hot water; drain. Toss with sauce. Serve with a bowl of Parmesan cheese on the side.

Linguine with Clam Sauce (J. Spina)

Ingredients	4 portions	Method
Clams, chopped	2 6½-oz. cans	Open clams; strain juice into a bowl; reserve separately.
Olive oil	5 Tbsp.	Sauté until brown.
Green onions, tops removed, minced	1 bunch	
Garlic cloves, pared, crushed	2	
Tomatoes, diced	1 No. 2½ can	Add with reserved clam juice. Simmer over low heat, stirring occasionally, for 30 minutes. Add reserved clams; cook for 2 minutes.
Tomato paste	1 tsp.	
Sweet basil	¼ tsp.	
Oregano	¼ tsp.	
Salt	to taste	
Pepper	to taste	
Linguine	1 lb.	Boil in 4 qt. rapidly boiling salted water for 12 minutes until al dente. Drain well; arrange on hot platter. Pour hot sauce over.
Vegetable oil	as needed	
Parmesan cheese	2 Tbsp.	Garnish with.
Parsley, minced	1 Tbsp.	

Rice Pilaf (M. Minor)

Ingredients	5-6 portions	Method
Water, hot	2¼ cups	Combine in heavy 2 or 2½ qt. saucepan. Heat to boiling, stirring until well blended.
Butter	4 Tbsp.	
Prepared French onion soup base	1¾ oz.	
Prepared consommè base	1 tsp.	
Long grain enriched parboiled rice, uncooked	1 cup	Stir in; cover tightly. Reduce heat to simmer and gently boil for 25 minutes until tender. Remove from heat. Let stand covered until all liquid is absorbed, for about 5 minutes. Serve hot.

VEGETABLES

Colorful vegetables add excitement (from top) Broccoli Timbale, Bavarian Red Cabbage,
Vegetables with the Oriental Touch and Swiss Skillet Potato Cake.

New kinds of vegetables, new varieties of the vegetables we have always known, are constantly coming into use. With this century's new knowledge of nutrition, vitamins and minerals, and the need for trace elements, we are coming to understand nutritional values. There are gourmet pleasures to be found in cooking and eating vegetables.

The successful chef and cook today must know about scores of vegetables, some newly developed. The chef must know what looks and tastes best and also how and when to serve them with appropriate entrees.

The modern chefs treat vegetables with a new respect and study how to preserve their delicate, sensitive nutrients and flavors. The old English system of boiling vegetables to death is no longer viable.

There are seven classifications of vegetables:

–Root vegetables—beets, carrots, turnips, knob celery, parsnips, salsify or oyster plant.

–Fruit vegetables—eggplants, cucumbers, squash, zucchini, green and red peppers, and tomatoes.

–Green and leafy vegetables—celery stalks, chicory, cabbage, brussel sprouts, kale, Swiss chard, broccoli and mustard greens.

–Thistle vegetables—asparagus, artichokes, cardoon.

–Bulbous vegetables—garlic, onion, shallot, leek and fennel.

–Tuberous vegetables—Jerusalem artichokes, potatoes, yams and carrots.

–Grains or dry beans—peas, green and yellow lentils.

Vegetables are cooked by blanching, braising, steaming, stir-frying and sautéeing.

—Hermann Rusch

Vegetables with the Oriental Touch (S. Krauss)

Ingredients	4 portions	Method
Sesame seed oil	1 oz.	Heat oil in sauté pan; add butter.
Butter	2 oz.	
Leek, cleaned, julienne	3 oz.	Add; sauté for 2 to 3 minutes.
Large carrot, pared, julienne	1	
Zucchini, julienne	3 oz.	
Celery ribs, julienne	4	
Small onion, pared, julienne	1	
Nutmeg	to taste	
Salt	to taste	
White pepper	to taste	
Green onions	2	Serve on platter; garnish with green onions.

Swiss Skillet Potato Cake (J. Kosec)

Ingredients	4 portions	Method
New potatoes, cooked, pared	1 lb.	Shred potatoes; add salt and chives.
Chives	2 Tbsp.	
Salt	½ tsp.	
Eggs, lightly beaten	3	Mix.
Light or heavy cream	¼ cup	
Parmesan cheese, grated	¼ cup	
Swiss cheese, grated	¼ cup	
Salt	½ tsp.	
Pepper	½ tsp.	
Butter	¼ cup	Heat butter in 10-in. skillet over medium heat. Add potatoes to cover bottom evenly. Pour egg mixture over it; cook for about 15 minutes or until potatoes are brown. Invert potato cakes in skillet; cook for about 10 minutes.
Parsley, chopped	3 Tbsp.	Remove to round dish; cut into wedges. Garnish with chopped parsley; serve hot.

Broccoli Timbale (K. Sehl)

Ingredients	6 portions	Method
Broccoli, cleaned	11 oz.	Cut broccoli into florets; cut stems into very thin slices. Place in casserole; heat to boiling; cover. Steam for 5 minutes. Remove cover; let liquid evaporate. Chop broccoli very fine in food processor.
Butter	½ oz.	
Chicken stock	6½ oz.	
Salt	to taste	
White pepper	to taste	
Nutmeg	to taste	
Egg yolks	2	Add while processor is running.
Heavy cream	1¾ oz.	
Egg whites, beaten until soft peaks form	2	Place in buttered timbale forms in shallow water bath. Bake at 350F for 20 to 25 minutes. If top starts to brown, cover with aluminum foil.

Bavarian Red Cabbage (K. Habich)

Ingredients	6 portions	Method
Medium head red cabbage	1	Mix.
Apples, cored, sliced	3	
Medium onion, pared, sliced	1	
Vinegar	⅓ cup	
Red wine	⅕ cup	Add; sauté for 1½ hours.
Water	⅘ cup	
Sugar	¼ cup	
Cloves	2	
Bay leaf	1	
Nutmeg, freshly grated	to taste	
Salt	to taste	
Pepper	to taste	
Lemon, juice of	½	
Medium potato, pared, cooked, grated	1	Mix; add.
Butter	2 Tbsp.	

Cauliflower Torte (W. Kaemer)

Ingredients	4 portions	Method
Puff pastry dough, frozen	1 sheet	Place in 10-in. round cake pan.
Large cauliflower heads	2	Break into florets. Cook for 20 minutes; reserve stock.
Ham, medium dice	12 oz.	Arrange, with florets, over pastry.
Parsley, chopped	¼ cup	
Eggs, beaten	8	Mix well. Pour over cauliflower mixture.
White wine	1 cup	
Reserved cauliflower stock	1 cup	
Swiss cheese, shredded	5 oz.	
Flour, all-purpose	¼ cup	
Nutmeg	to taste	
Salt	to taste	
Pepper	to taste	
Butter	3 oz.	Dot over torte. Bake at 375F for 45 minutes.

Potato Kugel

(A. Cline)

Ingredients	6-8 portions	Method
Large potatoes, pared	5	Grate, using fine blade; drain well; squeeze dry.
Large onion, pared, grated	1	Add; combine well. Pour into well-oiled, warm baking dish or glass casserole. Bake at 400F for 1 hour or until crust is brown. Serve hot.
Large eggs	3	
Chicken fat, melted	½ cup	
Matzo meal	⅓ cup	
Salt	1 tsp.	
White pepper	¼ tsp.	
Cinnamon	¼ tsp.	
Nutmeg	¼ tsp.	

Eggplant Parmigiana Alla Napoletana

(J. Spina)

Ingredients	4-6 portions	Method
Tomato purée	2 lb., 8 oz.	Combine; heat in well-heated saucepan over medium heat for about 20 minutes (be careful not to scorch); reserve.
Tomato paste	1 Tbsp.	
Parsley, chopped	1 Tbsp.	
Sweet basil, ground	½ tsp.	
Oregano, ground	½ tsp.	
Garlic cloves, pared, chopped	2	
Salt	to taste	
Pepper	to taste	
Large eggplant, pared, cut into ½-in.-thick slices	1	Place slices on rack; sprinkle lightly with salt; let stand for about 20 minutes so bitter juice can run off. Rinse each slice; pat dry with paper toweling. Coat each slice with flour; dip in egg; then coat lightly with bread crumbs.
Salt	as needed	
Flour	1 cup	
Eggs, beaten	3	
Bread crumbs	2 cups	
Olive oil	¾ cup	Heat oil in heavy skillet (oil should be ½-in. deep). When oil is hot, add eggplant slices. Heat 2 minutes on each side or until soft and golden. Reserve slices on paper toweling to absorb excess oil. Place about ½-in. of reserved tomato sauce over bottom of baking dish. Place eggplant in layers in dish; sprinkle each layer with cheeses; alternate layers until all ingredients are used, reserving a little of each cheese for top. Cover lightly with remaining sauce and reserved cheeses. Bake at 325F for 30 minutes.
Mozzarella cheese, shredded	8 oz.	
Parmesan cheese, grated	½ cup	

Artichokes and Mushrooms A La Grecque

(J. Deluhery)

Ingredients	10 portions	Method
Artichoke bottoms, cut into quarters	24	Combine; simmer until tender. Let cool in stock. Strain stock; serve very cold.
Large mushrooms	24	
White wine	1 pt.	
Capers	1 cup	
Olive oil	½ cup	
Lemons, juice of	3	
Coriander seeds	3	
Bay leaf	1	
Salt	pinch	
Fennel	pinch	
Thyme	pinch	
Chervil	pinch	

Zucchini Puffs

(F. Sgro)

Ingredients	8 portions	Method
Bread crumbs	½ cup	Combine.
Milk	½ cup	
Water	½ cup	
Medium zucchini, shredded	1	
Eggs	2	
Romano or Parmesan cheese, grated	to taste	
Parsley, chopped	to taste	
Basil	to taste	
Flour	1 cup	Mix thoroughly into egg mixture. Drop by table-spoonfuls into hot oil. Heat on both sides until brown. Drain on paper toweling. Serve as side dish or hors d'oeuvre.
Baking soda	¼ tsp.	
Salt	Pinch	

Stuffed Eggplant Padovana

(S. Sabatelle)

Ingredients	2 portions	Method
Medium eggplant	1	Clean eggplant; cut in half lengthwise. Scoop out pulp, leaving shell ½-in. thick. Cut pulp into small pieces.
Medium onion, pared, minced	1	Combine with pulp. Fill eggplant halves with mixture.
Parsley, chopped	1 Tbsp.	
Celery, chopped	2 Tbsp.	
Small green pepper, chopped	1	
Plum tomatoes	1 cup	
Bread crumbs	1 cup	
Imported cheese, grated	¼ cup	
Salt	to taste	
Pepper	to taste	
Imported olive oil	3 Tbsp.	Place in baking dish with eggplant. Bake at 350F for 45 minutes (lower heat if necessary to prevent browning).

Parisian Style Green Beans

(J. Piskor)

Ingredients	10 portions	Method
Water	1 gal.	Heat to boiling.
Salt	3 tsp.	
Green beans, fresh cut	2 lb.	Place beans in boiling water; heat to boiling. Reduce heat; cook until tender. Drain in colander.
Butter	2 oz.	Heat butter in saucepan until melted. Add onions; cook for 4 to 5 minutes or until onions are translucent. Remove from heat.
Onions, pared, minced	2 cups	
Paprika	2 Tbsp.	Stir in until onions are well coated.
Flour	4 Tbsp.	Mix flour and sour cream. Add salt. Add to onion mixture. Simmer over low heat, stirring, for 4 to 5 minutes or until sauce is smooth. Gently stir in beans; cook until beans are thoroughly heated.
Sour cream	2 cups	
Salt	1 tsp.	

Roesti Potatoes

Ingredients	4-6 portions	Method
Potatoes, unpared	1½ lb.	Boil or steam potatoes until barely done. Let cool; pare; shred.
Salt	1 tsp.	Add; lightly mix in (do not stir potatoes).
Butter, clarified	3 Tbsp.	Heat butter in well-seasoned 10-in. nonstick skillet until haze forms. Place potatoes in skillet; pat down to form a cake. When potatoes begin to sizzle, reduce heat to very low; cover potatoes with lid or inverted serving platter (cover should touch potatoes). Cook potatoes over low heat for about 20 minutes. Turn over; serve (potatoes should be brown and crusty).

Broccoli Romano

(R. Soeder)

Ingredients	4 portions	Method
Flour Garlic salt White pepper	½ cup ½ tsp. pinch	Mix.
Eggs, beaten Cheese, grated	3 ½ cup	Mix.
Broccoli, frozen or fresh, cooked crisp-tender, drained	1 lb.	Dip broccoli in flour mixture; then in egg mixture.
Olive or vegetable oil	1 cup	Heat oil in skillet; heat broccoli in skillet until brown on both sides. Heat broccoli at 450F for 8 to 10 minutes. Serve as side dish or with pasta. Sprinkle with grated cheese before serving.

Eggplant Parmigiana

(S. Sabatelle)

Ingredients	10 portions	Method
Large eggplant, pared, sliced Salt	1 as needed	Sprinkle each slice with salt; place in colander. Place weight on top; let stand for 1 hour.
Olive oil Onion, pared, minced Parsley sprigs, minced Garlic clove, pared, crushed	2 Tbsp. ½ 2 1	Heat in saucepan until onion is golden.
Italian plum-style tomatoes Salt Pepper	1 No. 2 can to taste to taste	Add; simmer over low heat for 1 hour.
Egg, beaten Flour Olive oil	1 1 cup ¼ cup	Thoroughly rinse eggplant; squeeze out all water. Dip each slice in egg; then in flour; sauté in oil.
Parmesan cheese, grated	1 cup	Arrange layers of fried eggplant, sauce and cheese, ending with sauce and cheese on top. Bake at 350F for 30 minutes or until brown.

VEGETABLES

Eggplant Caviar
(H. Bendixen)

Ingredients	4 portions	Method
Medium eggplants	5	Sear skin of eggplants over open gas flame; let cool in ice water. When cool, remove skin; drain pulp in colander.
Green peppers Vegetable oil	2 as needed	Heat whole peppers in oil in deep-fryer until crisp-tender. Let cool. When cool, remove skin and seeds. Mince. When eggplant is drained, mince; add.
Onion, pared, minced Olive oil Mayonnaise Lemons, juice of Salt White pepper	½ cup 3 Tbsp. 3 Tbsp. 3 1 tsp. ¼ tsp.	Add; combine well.

Baked Mushrooms
(G. Shaffer)

Ingredients	4 portions	Method
Mushrooms, sliced Lemon juice	8 oz. 2 Tbsp.	Sprinkle mushrooms with lemon juice. Place in small saucepan.
Butter Parmesan cheese, freshly grated Flour, all-purpose Onion, pared, minced Salt Black pepper, freshly ground	2 Tbsp. 2 Tbsp. 1 Tbsp. 1 Tbsp. ¼ tsp. to taste	Add; stir to mix; simmer, covered, for 3 minutes. Transfer to baking dish.
Heavy cream Egg yolks, lightly beaten	1 cup 2	Mix; pour over mushroom mixture.
Fine bread crumbs, fresh Butter	2 Tbsp. 2 Tbsp.	Sprinkle bread crumbs over dish; dot with butter. Bake at 425F for 10 minutes or until golden.

Potato Pancakes
(C. Wendt)

Ingredients	4 portions	Method
Idaho potatoes, pared, grated Onions, pared, minced Eggs, whole Flour Parsley, fresh, minced Salt White pepper	4 ½ lb. 4 5 oz. 1 oz. pinch pinch	Combine well; shape mixture into 4-in. pancakes.
Vegetable oil or clarified butter	1 pt.	Place oil in wide skillet. Heat pancakes until browned on both sides. Drain on paper toweling. Keep warm. Serve with applesauce or sour cream.

Onion Pie

(R. Ebert)

Ingredients	6 portions	Method
Onions, pared, chopped	2 cups	Sauté until tender.
Butter or margarine	½ cup	
Flour	¼ cup	Add to make roux.
Light cream	1 cup	Add; let cool for 10 to 15 minutes.
Salt	1 tsp.	
White pepper	¼ tsp.	
Eggs, lightly beaten	2	Add.
Prepared pie shells, 9-in.	2	Pour mixture into pie shell. Cover with remaining pie shell. Brush with egg wash. Bake at 375F for 45 to 50 minutes.
Egg wash	as needed	

Broccoli Alla Romana

(J. Piskor)

Ingredients	6-8 portions	Method
Broccoli	2 lb.	Cut off stalks; thoroughly wash broccoli in cold water.
Olive oil	½ cup	Heat oil in heavy skillet until light haze forms.
Garlic, pared, chopped	2 tsp.	Remove skillet from heat; place garlic in hot oil for 30 seconds. Return to moderate heat. Add broccoli; toss until coated with oil.
White wine	3 cups	Add; simmer, uncovered, stirring occasionally, for 10 minutes. Simmer, covered, for 15 minutes or until broccoli is tender but firm. Place broccoli on heated platter. Heat cooking liquid to boiling; boil until reduced by half. Pour liquid over broccoli; serve.
Salt	1 tsp.	
Black pepper	¼ tsp.	

Spinach Pudding

(A. Valdez)

Ingredients	10 portions	Method
Spinach, cooked, minced	2 cups	Combine.
Bread crumbs	2 cups	
Light cream	1 cup	
Eggs, beaten	3	
Butter	2 Tbsp.	
Salt	½ tsp.	
Pepper	⅛ tsp.	
Onion juice	to taste	
Butter	as needed	Spread butter over cloth napkin; sprinkle with bread crumbs. Cover with spinach mixture; roll up. Tie with string all around and at ends. Steam for 30 minutes. When done, remove from napkin. Cut into 2-in.-long slices; roll out before serving.
Fine bread crumbs	as needed	

VEGETABLES

Sweet Potato Pone
(J. Deluhery)

Ingredients	10 portions	Method
Sweet potatoes, medium, unpared	2 lb.	Boil for about 1 hour or until tender. Remove skins; mash pulp. Beat until smooth.
Brown sugar	¾ cup	Add; stir to blend thoroughly.
Eggs, beaten	3	
Nutmeg	¼ tsp.	
Cinnamon	¼ tsp.	
Salt	¼ tsp.	
Evaporated milk	1 cup	Pour into greased casserole.
Butter, melted	¼ cup	
Pecans, coarsely chopped	6 oz.	Sprinkle over top. Bake at 325F for about 1½ hours or until done.

Chilies Rellenos
(R. Marshall)

Ingredients	8 portions	Method
Monterey Jack cheese, cut into long, narrow, pie-shaped stripes or wedges	8 oz.	Place strip of cheese in each chili; dust completely with flour; refrigerate until thoroughly chilled.
Green chilies, canned	8	
Flour	2 Tbsp.	
Eggs, separated	4	Beat egg whites and cream of tartar until stiff peaks form. Beat egg yolks and salt until thoroughly combined. Add to egg white mixture; lightly sprinkle flour over mixtures; lightly fold together.
Cream of tartar	¼ tsp.	
Salt	¼ tsp.	
Flour	as needed	
Vegetable oil	as needed	Dip each chili in batter until well covered with batter; cover any bare spots with batter. Place chilies in about ½ in. of hot oil in large skillet. Immediately turn chilies; continue heating until both sides are golden (do not crowd in pan). Drain on paper toweling.
Chilies Rellenos Sauce	recipe follows	Serve hot, plain or with sauce.

Chilies Rellenos Sauce
(R. Marshall)

Ingredients	8 portions	Method
Salt	½ tsp.	Crush garlic with salt.
Garlic clove, pared	1	
Onion, pared, diced or sliced	1 cup	Combine; add; heat until soft.
Green bell pepper, diced or sliced	1 cup	
Fat or oil	2 Tbsp.	
Chicken or pork broth or water	4 cups	Add; cook for 5 minutes.
Tomatoes, canned, mashed	2 cups	
Oregano, whole, rubbed between hands	1 tsp.	
White pepper	¼ tsp.	
Flour	3 Tbsp.	Mix flour and water until smooth; add to boiling sauce. Cook for 3 to 4 minutes or until thick. Serve with Chilies Rellenos.
Water	as needed	

NOTES

BREADS

Freshly baked products add a touch of goodness to menus: (clockwise from top) Yorkshire Pudding Popover, Wyoming Bran Muffins, Southern Breakfast Biscuits.

Bread in its simplest form is basically a baked dough of flour and water that is leavened by yeast. Some French breads include those ingredients and salt. Other breads have added ingredients: sugar, shortening, milk, eggs and flavorings. But the basic building blocks are flour, water and yeast.

Still, bread can be one of the most difficult products to make. Successful bread making depends largely on understanding two basic principles: gluten development and yeast fermentation.

Quick breads are the inexpensive, low-labor alternative to yeast breads. They also have the advantage of being made with many ingredients, allowing for the creation of a signature bread.

Knowing about flour is important in bread production. Weather conditions and type of flour can considerably change the end product. Three basic flours are used in bread: white-wheat flour, whole-wheat flour and rye flour.

White wheat flour is milled from wheat kernels after the outer covering and the germ have been removed. Bakers select flour on the basis of its gluten content. High-protein flours are called strong; low-protein flours are called weak. There are three basic types of white-wheat flour:

–Bread flour—a strong flour that is used for making breads, hard rolls and any other high-gluten product. The best bread flours are called patents.

–Cake flour—a weak or low-gluten flour made from soft wheat. It has a very soft texture and is a pure white color. It is used for cakes and other delicate baked goods.

–Pastry flour—lower in gluten than bread flour but higher than cake flour. It has the same creamy white color as bread flour. It is used for cookies, pie pastry, biscuits, muffins and some sweet yeast doughs.

Whole-wheat flour is made by grinding the entire wheat kernel. It contains gluten and so can be used by itself to make bread, although it produces a heavy product. Graham flour is whole-wheat flour in which the bran has been ground very fine.

Rye flour does not develop gluten, so it must be used in combination with other flours. It is available in light, medium and dark shades.

Other flours such as soy, potato, oat and barley do not develop gluten, and so must be used with a wheat flour.   —*Lutz Olkiewicz*

Southern Breakfast Biscuits (A. Ausserlechner)

Ingredients	12 portions	Method
Flour, sifted Baking powder Salt	9 oz. 1½ oz. 2 oz.	Mix together.
Shortening	8 oz.	Add. Gently rub in until sandy consistency.
Buttermilk	8 oz.	Make well in center; pour in. Fold together slowly. Place onto floured surface and fold to ¼-in. to ½-in. thickness. Cut out with 2½-in.-diameter pastry cutter. Place on buttered baking sheet. Bake at 450F for 5-6 minutes. Brush with melted butter when done. Serve stuffed with ham, egg or sausage.

Bishop's Christmas Bread (F. Ambrose)

Ingredients	1 large loaf or 2 small loaves	Method
Eggs	3	Beat well.
Sugar	1 cup	Add gradually; mix well.
Flour Salt Baking powder	1¼ cups, 1 tsp. ½ tsp. 1½ tsp.	Mix together.
Maraschino cherries Walnuts, coarsely chopped Dates, chopped Minichocolate chips	1 cup 1 cup 1 cup 1 cup	Add to dry ingredients. Add fruit-flour mixture to egg mixture; blend quickly and thoroughly. Pour into greased loaf pans, one 5½-x-9½-in. pan or two 3½-x-5½-in. pans. Bake large loaf at 350F for 1 hour; bake small loaves at 350F for 50 minutes.

Yorkshire Pudding-Popover (B. Urban)

Ingredients	12 portions	Method
Eggs	6	Place in mixing bowl; beat at medium speed.
Milk, heated	1 qt.	Add while continuing beating.
Flour, sifted	18 oz.	Add a little at a time, reduce speed to slow while adding.
Salt	½ tsp.	Add.
White pepper	¼ tsp.	
Nutmeg	¼ tsp.	
Ground beef suet	12 oz.	Place 1 oz. in each tin; render in hot 400F oven. Do not burn. Fill tins ¾ full with batter; return to oven; bake for 10-15 minutes at 400F or until batter has popped. Reduce oven to 325F; bake for an additional 30 minutes.

Wyoming Bran Muffins (J. Lucero)

Ingredients	10-12 portions	Method
Bread flour	4 oz.	Combine in 4-qt. bowl.
Sugar	4 oz.	
Bakers bran	2 oz.	
Baking soda	⅛ tsp.	
Baking powder	⅛ tsp.	
Salt	⅛ tsp.	
Buttermilk	1 cup	Add; mix well.
Eggs, beaten	2	
Butter, melted	2 oz.	
Dates, chopped	2 oz.	
Raisins	4 oz.	
Oil	1 Tbsp.	Coat tins.
Flour	½ cup	
Walnuts, coarsely chopped	¾ cup	Add 1 heaping Tbsp. in bottom of each tin.
Honey	⅛ cup	Mix well. Add 1 tsp. to bottom of each tin. Divide bran mixture equally among tins. Bake at 400F for 25 minutes. Remove muffins while still warm.
Shortening	1 oz.	
Brown sugar	2 oz.	
Sugar	2 oz.	

Alabama Mush Bread (W.C. O'Neill)

Ingredients	10 portions	Method
White or yellow cornmeal	2 cups	Cook cornmeal in water until done.
Boiling water	2 cups	
Milk	1 cup	Add; mix well. Turn into well-greased 10-in. skillet; sprinkle cornmeal on bottom. Let cook on top of range until bread is brown on the bottom. Bake at 400F until bread is brown on top. Turn out on large platter; cut in wedge-shaped pieces.
Egg	1	
Salt	½ tsp.	
Butter or margarine	2 Tbsp.	
Flour	2 cups	

Banana Nut Bread

(R. Ebert)

Ingredients	3 8½x4½ loaves	Method
Flour	7 cups	Sift together.
Baking powder	5 tsp.	
Salt	2 tsp.	
Sugar	3 cups	Cream together; add.
Shortening	1⅓ cups	
Eggs	8	Add; combine thoroughly.
Vanilla	2 tsp.	
Bananas, very ripe, mashed	4 cups	Add.
Chopped nuts	1½ cups	Add; pour into 8½x4½-in. loaf pans. Bake at 350F for 1 hour, 10 minutes or until wooden pick inserted comes out clean.

German Onion Cake

(W. Kraemer)

Ingredients	4 portions	Method
Flour	4 oz.	Place in large mixing bowl.
Dry yeast	1 oz.	Dissolve yeast, sugar and salt in milk. Add.
Sugar	1 tsp.	
Salt	pinch	
Milk	4 oz.	
Butter, softened	1½ oz.	Blend in. Mix until dough comes off bottom of bowl. Cover with damp cloth; let sit for 30 minutes.
Water	3 Tbsp.	
Lean bacon, ½-in. strips	4 oz.	Sauté until light brown.
Raw onion, sliced	1 lb.	Add to bacon; sauté until golden. Place dough in 10-in. pie pan; add onion mixture.
Eggs	3	Mix; pour over onion mixture. Place in preheated 375F oven; bake for 35-40 minutes. Serve warm.
Sour cream	5 oz.	
Caraway seeds, ground	¼ tsp.	
Salt	to taste	

Tarheel Corn Muffins

(A. Ausserlechner)

Ingredients	1 dozen	Method
Butter	4 oz.	Heat until melted; reserve.
Flour, sifted	6 oz.	Combine.
Cornmeal	1½ oz.	
Sugar	1½ oz.	
Baking powder	½ oz.	
Salt	½ oz.	
Eggs, beaten	2	Fold in until smooth.
Buttermilk	8 oz.	Add with reserved butter. Pour mixture ¾ of the way up the sides of a greased muffin pan. Bake at 400F for 6 minutes or until fully risen and golden.

Hanky-panky Pancakes   (H. Bazan)

Ingredients	6 portions	Method
Eggs	2	Beat in large bowl.
Beer	12 oz.	Add.
Vegetable oil, margarine or bacon fat, melted	4 Tbsp.	
Sugar	2 Tbsp.	
Flour, sifted	4 cups	Combine in sifter; add. Drop from ice cream scoop onto hot griddle or skillet. Heat until bubbles form; turn over. Serve with warm maple syrup and butter.
Baking powder	4 tsp.	

Hush Puppies   (O. Sommers)

Ingredients	6 portions	Method
Cornmeal	2 cups	Combine.
Flour	1 Tbsp.	
Baking powder	1 tsp.	
Baking soda	1 tsp.	
Salt	1 tsp.	
White pepper	pinch	
Buttermilk	1½ cups	Combine; add; combine thoroughly. Drop from No. 40 ice cream scoop into deep hot fat (375F). Deep-fry as many as will float uncrowded in a layer, turning with a fork several times (do not pierce), for 3 to 4 minutes or until brown. Remove with slotted spoon; drain on paper toweling.
Onion, pared, chopped	⅓ cup	
Egg, well beaten	1	

French Bread   (M. Minor)

Ingredients	3 1-lb. loaves	Method
Water, lukewarm	2 cups	Combine; let stand for 3 to 5 minutes. Whisk with wire whisk until yeast is completely dissolved.
Cake yeast	2 oz.	
Sugar	¾ oz.	
Shortening	¼ cup	Add; combine thoroughly.
Salt	3½ tsp.	
Bread flour	7 cups	Gradually add flour, scraping down bowl twice. Continue adding flour until dough cleans side of mixer bowl; mix for 5 minutes. Cover with plastic wrap and wet towel. Let rise in warm place until doubled in size; punch down dough; let rise again. Repeat 2 times. Cut dough into 1-lb. pieces. Roll out dough into rectangular shape; roll tightly into French loaf.
Cornmeal	as needed	Place loaf on pan dusted with cornmeal. Let rise for 2 hours or until doubled in size. Bake at 375F for 40 minutes. Brush with eggwash; bake for 7 minutes. Remove from pan; refrigerate.
Eggwash	as needed	

NOTES

DESSERTS

Elegant desserts from the culinary crème de la crème: (clockwise from l.) Mocha Chiffon Pie, Pears in Red Wine and Bananas Flambé in Rum-Raisin Sauce.

The successful introduction of pastries—not only in France, but in Switzerland, Austria, Germany and all the other Western European countries—started with the introduction of the beet sugar. Beet sugar became the immediate reason for successful pastry business. Once beet sugar was available, sweets were not only available for royalty and nobility, but also for the common man.

For instance, in Germany, there is a guild that has existed for over 400 years and is closely related to the pastry field. It produced all the items for Christmas including honey doughs.

The development goes as follows: With the introduction of beet sugar in Europe and the availability of beet sugar, bakeries tended to produce sweet breads and cakes as well as a variety of sweet desserts. They became very successful and already at the end of the 1800s these shops added extra room to bakeries. They gave a version of superb elegance and excellence of fine pasteries, desserts, cakes, puddings, candies and tortes that we still enjoy today. **—Lutz Olkiewicz**

Almond Stuffed Peaches (J. Kosec)

Ingredients	6 portions	Method
Fresh peach halves or canned peach halves	6	Pare and seed; place on dish.
Almonds, toasted	2 oz.	Pulverize in chopper or with French knife until mealy.
Powdered sugar	1½ oz.	Add to almonds in blender.
Sherry	½ oz.	Add to almonds; blend. Stuff peaches. Place peaches in casserole dish.
Powdered sugar	6 tsp.	Sprinkle over peaches.
Dry sherry	½ cup	Add to casserole dish. Bake at 350F for 15-20 minutes for fresh peaches, 10 minutes for canned. Serve in champagne glass warm with wine from casserole dish.

Glazed Pears (D. Jaramillo)

Ingredients	20 portions	Method
Fresh Bartlett pears, unpared	20	Cut off bottoms, leaving stems on.
Lemon juice	¼ cup	Add to large bowl of water; add pears to prevent browning.
Water	6 cups	Combine in saucepan large enough to hold pears. Heat, stirring until sugar dissolves. Heat to boiling; add pears. Cover; simmer for about 15 minutes, removing cover now and then to turn and baste pears with liquid. Cook just until pears are barely tender. Remove pears; boil syrup rapidly to reduce and thicken slightly.
Sugar	4 cups	
Lemon juice	¾ cup	
Vanilla	2 tsp.	
Cornstarch	1 tsp.	Mix; stir into reduced syrup. Simmer a minute, stirring until sauce is clear and slightly thickened. Remove from heat.
Cold water	1 Tbsp.	
Orange-flavored liqueur	2 Tbsp.	Stir in. Make three spiral-shaped slashes in each pear. Spoon sauce slowly over pears. Cool.

Bananas Flambé in Rum-Raisin Sauce
(S. Krauss)

Ingredients	12 portions	Method
Sweet butter	½ cup	Heat flambé pan over flame. Place butter in pan to melt.
Brown sugar	1 cup	Add; stir until it becomes a smooth syrup.
Bananas, green tipped	6	Cut lengthwise. Add to syrup; baste.
Ground cloves	pinch	Add.
Mace	pinch	
Golden raisins	½ cup	
Cinnamon	pinch	
Nutmeg	pinch	
Vanilla extract	½ tsp.	
Banana liqueur	½ cup	Pour over banana mixture; allow to heat. Ignite (might ignite without match, take caution). Move pan back and forth over flame.
Rum, 151 proof	1 cup	
French vanilla ice cream	1 qt.	Spoon bananas and sauce over ice cream in individual dishes.
Whipping cream	2 cups	Whip together.
Powdered sugar	½ cup	
Red maraschino cherries	12	Decorate banana topped ice cream.
Almonds, sliced, dyed with green food color	garnish	

Mocha Chiffon Pie
(F. Lozier)

Ingredients	6-8 portions	Method
Cold water	2½ Tbsp.	Dissolve gelatin by sprinkling on water; mix. Reserve.
Unflavored gelatin	1 Tbsp.	
Milk	3 Tbsp.	Dissolve starch in milk; reserve.
Cornstarch	3 Tbsp.	
Water	1 cup	Combine in saucepan. Heat to boiling. Add gelatin mixture; stir until dissolved.
Chocolate	1 oz.	
Sugar	6 Tbsp.	
Salt	¼ tsp.	
Heavy cream	3 Tbsp.	Stir into chocolate mixture.
Vanilla	1 tsp.	
Egg whites	3	Whip egg whites to a foam; gradually add sugar. Continue whipping to soft peak. Fold hot mixture into meringue mixture.
Sugar	6 Tbsp.	
Prepared graham cracker pie crust, 9-in.	1	Pour mixture into crust; let cool at room temperature.
Heavy cream	1 cup	Whip to a firm peak.
Sugar	2 Tbsp.	
Instant granulated coffee	1 tsp.	Mix together; fold into whipped cream. Top pie with whipped cream. Decorate with shaved or curled sweet chocolate.
Hot water	1 tsp.	

Mozartkuppel (F. Buck)

Ingredients	8-10 portions	Method
Eggs	4	Beat over steam until warm and thick.
Sugar	4 oz.	
Vanilla sugar	1 tsp.	Add; continue beating.
Lemon rind, grated	to taste	
Flour	4 oz.	Mix in.
Butter, melted	1.5 oz.	Stir in. Butter a cone-shaped cake mold; sprinkle with flour. Put dough into mold; bake at 360F for 1 hour. Turn upside down when cool. Cut into seven parallel layers.
Sour cherry juice	5 Tbsp.	Mix. Sprinkle over cake layers.
Rum	2 Tbsp.	
Heavy cream	1 cup	Combine. Spread between layers of cake.
Confectioners' sugar	1 oz.	
Vanilla sugar	1 tsp.	
Sour cherries, pits removed	7 oz.	
Rum	1 Tbsp.	
Heavy cream	½ cup	Heat cream to boiling; remove from heat. Add chocolate; stir until smooth. Cool at room temperature; stir until creamy. Spread over cone-shaped cake. Garnish with cocktail cherries and marzipan roses.
Bittersweet chocolate	4 oz.	

Zesty Lemon Meringue Pie (H. Carruthers)

Ingredients	7 portions	Method
Lemons, rind and juice of	3	Grate rind of 2 lemons into sugar.
Sugar	1 cup	
Cornstarch	4 Tbsp.	Dissolve cornstarch in only enough water to make a paste.
Water	as needed	
Egg yolks	3	Mix in with cornstarch.
Water	2 cups	Combine with sugar-lemon mixture and reserved juice in saucepan; heat to boiling. Add cornstarch mixture and yolks; cook and stir until thickened. Remove from heat; allow to cool.
Butter or margarine	1 Tbsp.	
Prepared pie shell, 9-in. baked	1	Fill with lemon mixture.
Egg whites	3	Beat eggs at high speed until peaks form; gradually add sugar. Continue to whip until stiff peaks form. Allow filling to completely cool before applying meringue. Dust with confectioners' sugar; place in 400F oven to color.
Confectioners' sugar	6 Tbsp.	

Tofu-Cottage Cheese Cake
(J. Joaquin)

Ingredients	10 portions	Method
Cottage cheese, low-fat, small curd	1 lb.	Combine, mixing at medium speed of mixer until well blended.
Sugar	¾ cup	
Tofu, firm, strained	12 oz.	
Egg yolks	4	
Flour	4 Tbsp.	
Lemon rind, grated	1 tsp.	
Vanilla extract	1 tsp.	
Salt	¼ tsp.	
Cinnamon	¼ tsp.	
Gelatin	1 Tbsp.	
Egg whites	4	Beat together until stiff. Fold little at a time into cheese mixture.
Cream of tartar	¼ tsp.	
Cake crumbs, buttered	as needed	Line springform pan. Pour cake mixture into pan. Bake at 450F for 10 minutes. Reduce to 250F; continue baking for 40-50 minutes. Cool before removing rim from pan; refrigerate. Spread with preserves and top with whipping cream.

Cold Lemon Tequila Soufflé
(G. Preuss)

Ingredients	6 portions	Method
Sugar	⅔ cup	Mix together in saucepan; heat to boiling. Boil gently until mixture begins to thicken. Remove; refrigerate.
Water	1 cup	
Lemon juice	2½ oz.	Add to cold sugar mixture. Cook over low heat, whisking constantly, until foam subsides. Place in refrigerator; stir occasionally to cool.
Egg yolks	6	
White wine	3 oz.	
Tequila	1½ oz.	
Whipped cream	1½ cup	Fold into cooled mixture. To serve, place soufflé in hollowed out lemons on bed of shaved ice; freeze. Garnish with whipped cream and mint leaf.

Bearclaw Cookies
(K. Eid)

Ingredients	1 dozen	Method
Almond paste	8 oz.	Combine.
Eggs	4	
Confectioners' sugar	8 oz.	Add; mix until it is a dough. Let rest for 24 hours. Scale off into 8 oz. pieces. Shape a roll; cut in 1-in. rounds.
Chocolate powder	2 oz.	
Cake crumbs	1 lb.	
Cinnamon	½ Tbsp.	
Cloves	½ tsp.	
Vanilla extract	1 Tbsp.	
Sugar	as needed	Press round in sugar. With sugar side down, shape into 1½-in. wooden bearclaw molds or shape by hand. Place on paper-lined baking sheets; bake at 375F for 10 minutes.
Milk chocolate coating	9 oz.	When cookies cool, dip in coating or brush coating on. Store in closed container.

Cottage Cheese Souffle

(K. Sehl)

Ingredients	16 portions	Method
Butter	1 cup	Cream butter with 1 cup sugar until light.
Sugar	1½ cups	
Cottage cheese	2 cups	Add; beat until smooth.
Lemon juice	2 Tbsp.	Mix in.
Vanilla	1 Tbsp.	
Eggs, separated	8	Beat in egg yolks; reserve whites.
Flour	½ cup	Blend in. Whip egg whites until soft peaks form. Gradually beat in remaining ½ cup sugar until stiff and glossy. Fold in cottage cheese mixture. Ladle 6 oz. into each of 16 buttered 8 oz. soufflé dishes. Bake at 325F in water bath for 25-30 minutes. Serve warm within 10 minutes or chilled with fruit.
Sour cream	2 cups	
Salt	½ tsp.	

Voyager Strawberry Yogurt Pie

(S. Muthofer)

Ingredients	6-8 portions	Method
Pecans, finely chopped	1½ cups	Combine; press into 9-in. pie plate. Bake at 450F for 6 minutes; cool; reserve.
Sugar	3 Tbsp.	
Butter	2 Tbsp.	
Frozen strawberries, thawed	1 lb.	Drain; reserve ¼ cup syrup.
Plain gelatin	1 Tbsp.	Soak in reserved syrup for about 5 minutes; heat to dissolve. Add to strawberries.
Plain yogurt	¾ cup	Stir in. Refrigerate until mixture begins to set.
Whipping cream	½ pt.	Combine; fold into strawberry mixture. Pour into pie shell. Refrigerate for several hours or freeze until firm. Serve frozen or thawed. Garnish with whipped cream.
Sugar	3 Tbsp.	

Frozen Tutti-Fruitti Pie

(J. Deluhery)

Ingredients	32 portions	Method
Eggs	6	Combine; whisk in double boiler for 15 minutes. Remove from heat; beat at high mixer speed until cool.
Sugar	8 oz.	
Gelatin powder	2 oz.	Stir in.
Glace cherries, chopped	4 oz.	Soak cherries in kirsch; add to egg mixture.
Kirsch	2 oz.	
Confectioners' sugar	8 oz.	Fold together; add to egg mixture.
Whipped cream	1 gal.	
Sponge cakes, prepared in pie tins, 9-in.	4	Divide filling mixture evenly to top 4 sponge cakes in pie tins.
Glace cherries, chopped	6 oz.	Sprinkle over pie tins; place in freezer overnight.
Almonds, chopped	3 oz.	
Pistachio nuts	2 oz.	

Zabaglione (J. Spina)

Ingredients	6 portions	Method
Egg yolks	6	Beat in top of double boiler.
Sugar	4 Tbsp.	Gradually add; continue beating until light lemon color and thoroughly blended.
Marsala or port	¾ cup	Add; beat thoroughly again. Place mixture over lower part of double boiler. Cook over boiling water for about 5 minutes, or until it begins to thicken, beating continuously. Do not allow custard to boil. Remove from heat immediately; pour into sherbet or parfait glasses.
Cinnamon	¼ tsp.	Sprinkle over custard.

Roulade (J. Joaquin)

Ingredients	6 portions	Method
Eggs	4	Beat with electric mixer in large bowl until very thick.
Sugar	¾ cup	Beat in 2 Tbsp. at a time until very thick.
Flour, sifted	⅔ cup	Sift several times together; fold into mixture.
Baking powder	¾ tsp.	
Anise extract	¼ tsp.	Add; mix well. Line a greased 15 x 10 x 1-in. jelly roll pan with waxed paper. Grease paper; dust lightly with flour. Pour batter evenly into pan. Bake at 400F for 12-15 minutes or until light brown; do not over-bake.
Lemon rind	1 tsp.	
Salt	¼ tsp.	
Confectioners' sugar	as needed	Spread a kitchen towel with a thin layer of confectioners' sugar. Remove cake from pan onto the towel, paper-side up. Carefully strip off waxed paper. Roll up cake starting on the long side of the towel. Cool; unroll carefully.
Rum or brandy	as needed	Moisten roll; spread with preserves. Roll up again; place on serving platter. sprinkle with confectioners' sugar.
Fruit preserves	as needed	

German Chocolate Pie (E. Mason)

Ingredients	2 pies	Method
Sugar	1 lb.	Combine; blend until smooth.
Cocoa	2 oz.	
Cake flour	2 oz.	
Evaporated milk	1 qt.	
Eggs	4	
Coconut flakes	5 oz.	Fold into egg mixture.
Pecan halves	4 oz.	
Butter, melted	5 oz.	
Prepared pie shells, 10-in.	2	Fill with chocolate filling; bake at 360F for 40-45 minutes. Refrigerate overnight; decorate with fresh whipped cream.

Rice a la Reine Maria (C. Richter)

Ingredients	6-8 portions	Method
Long-grain rice	4 oz.	Place into heavy aluminum pot or double boiler; cook until rice is done and all liquid is absorbed, stirring often. Keep covered while cooking. When finished, remove from heat.
Milk	1 qt.	
Salt	¼ tsp.	
Butter	1 oz.	
Lemon rind, yellow only	1 inch	
Small cinnamon stick	1	
Vanilla extract	2 tsp.	
Golden raisins	½ cup	
Sugar	½ cup	
Egg yolks	2	Blend; mix into cooked rice while still hot.
Orange-flavored liqueur	1 Tbsp.	
Candied pineapple ring, small dice	1	Add to rice mixture; refrigerate.
Stayman apples, pared, cored, sliced	3	Simmer slowly until apples are tender; refrigerate.
Water	as needed	
Sugar	2 Tbsp.	
Egg whites	3	Beat together until stiff peaks form. Form cold rice pudding into loaf or dish it is to be served on. Take apple slices out of juice; drain well. Place over rice pudding; cover with beaten egg whites. Sprinkle with confectioners' sugar. Bake at 450F for a few minutes to carmelize eggs.
Sugar	2 Tbsp.	
Cream of tartar	¼ tsp.	

Eggnog (B. Galand)

Ingredients	1 portion	Method
Milk	1 cup	Blend first 4 ingredients in blender; garnish with nutmeg.
Egg	1	
Vanilla extract	¼ tsp.	
Sugar substitute	to taste	
Nutmeg	dash	

Cheesecake Leon (L. Korstejens)

Ingredients	4 9-in. cakes	Method
Graham cracker crumbs	2 lb.	Combine; line bottom of 4 9-in. springform pans. Bake at 350F for 3 minutes.
Butter, melted	14 oz.	
Sugar	10 oz.	
Cream cheese, room temperature	7 lb.	Combine; mix well at low speed of mixer until smooth.
Sugar	3 lb., 12 oz.	
Powdered milk	9 oz.	
Flour	6 oz.	
Lemons, rind and juice of	4	
Eggs	1 qt., 4 oz.	Add in two stages. Scrape side and bottom of bowl after each addition.
Water, hot	1 qt.	Add. Pour cheese mixture into springform pans; place in water bath in 350F oven for 15 minutes. Reduce heat to 300F; bake for 1 hour, 45 minutes.

Almond Tart (O. Sommer)

Ingredients	10 portions	Method
Egg yolks, slightly beaten	3	Combine; beat until mixture is smooth.
Sugar	¾ cup	
Water	⅓ cup	
Heavy cream	2 cups	Stir in thoroughly; reserve.
Almonds, blanched, finely ground	1 cup	
Macaroons, crushed	¼ cup	
Almond extract	½ tsp.	
Orange rind, grated	1 Tbsp.	
Flour, sifted	2 cups	Mound on a pastry board. Make a well in center.
Sugar	¼ cup	Put sugar, eggs and butter in center of flour well. Work the center ingredients with fingers to a smooth paste. Quickly work in flour forming a smooth round ball. If dough seems too dry, add a few drops of water. Knead dough very lightly; wrap in waxed paper. Refrigerate for at least 1 hour before using. Line tart pan with dough. Pour filling into tart shell; bake at 350F for 1 hour. Cool tart; top with sweetened whipped cream and slivered almonds.
Egg yolks	4	
Butter, broken in pieces	½ cup	
Water, cold	as needed	

Pineapple Tea Punch (B. Galand)

Ingredients	4 portions	Method
Cold tea	3 cups	Combine; pour over ice cubes in a tall glass. Let stand 2-3 minutes; serve.
Pineapple juice, unsweetened	¾ cup	
Lemon juice	¼ cup	
Liquid sugar substitute	4 tsp.	

Grasshopper Pie (L. Korstejens)

Ingredients	2 9-in. pies	Method
Chocolate wafer crumbs	2 cups	Combine; line 2 9-in. pie plates.
Sugar	½ cup	
Butter, melted	4 Tbsp.	
Milk	3 cups	Heat to boiling.
Sugar	¼ cup	
Egg yolks	3	Add; beat well.
Sugar	¼ cup	
Gelatin, soaked in water	¾ tsp.	Add; refrigerate.
Egg whites	3	Combine; whip until stiff peaks form; fold into partially set gelatin.
Sugar	¼ cup	
Whipped cream	1 cup	
Mint-flavored liqueur	¼ cup	Add.
Chocolate-flavored liqueur	¼ cup	
Prepared pie shells, 9-in. baked	2	Pour in filling; refrigerate. finish with whipped cream and chocolate shavings.

Crepes Angelica

Ingredients	6 portions	Method
Flour	2 cups	Combine.
Sugar	5 Tbsp.	
Salt	pinch	
Eggs	5	Add eggs and ½ cup milk. Beat for 10 minutes at high speed; add the rest of the milk. Beat at low speed for 5 minutes.
Milk	1 cup	
Butter, clarified	2 Tbsp.	Fry ½ oz. crepe batter in hot 6-in. crepe pan lined with butter, brown both sides. Reserve warm.
Milk	1 qt.	Heat to boiling.
Sugar	1 lb.	
Gelatin	1 oz.	
Coconut	9 oz.	
Water	1 cup	Add; cook until thick. Cool at room temperature.
Cornstarch	1 oz.	
Egg yolks	4	Fold into filling; place a portion on each crepe. Roll crepe; top with pineapple or strawberry sauce.
Vanilla	½ oz.	

Pears in Red Wine

Ingredients	8 portions	Method
Large Bartlett pear halves	8	Place in sauté pan.
Red wine or light port	750 mL.	Add to pears; simmer for 10-15 minutes. Remove from heat; marinate in refrigerator for 12-15 hours. Remove pears from pan. Heat marinade to boiling.
Brown sugar	10 oz.	
Cloves	4	
Cinnamon sticks	2	
Allspice or cardamom	pinch	
Cornstarch	1½ oz.	Mix with a small amount water; add to marinade. Refrigerate until cool. Place pears on serving platter; pour sauce over.
Water	as needed	
Heavy cream, whipped	1 cup	Garnish with whipped cream and toasted almonds.
Almonds, sliced, toasted	1 oz.	

Maple Gaufrettes Chantilly

Ingredients	12 portions	Method
Butter	4 oz.	Combine; heat until butter is dissolved; remove from heat; let cool.
Sugar	4 oz.	
Maple syrup	4 oz.	
Lemon, juice of	½	Add; mix well. Drop by spoonful onto well-greased flat baking pan, approximately 4-in. apart. Bake at 350F for 3 minutes or until brown. Remove from oven; let sit for a few seconds. While hot, roll gaufrettes around wooden pegs. Remove when cold.
Lemon rind, grated	1	
Vanilla bean	1	
Cinnamon	to taste	
Salt	to taste	
Flour	2½ oz.	
Whipping cream	1 cup	Whip cream until stiff; add sugar and vanilla, blend well. Just before serving, fill gaufrettes with whipped cream.
Sugar	1½ oz.	
Vanilla extract	½ tsp.	

DESSERTS

Bienenstich   (H. Warren)

Ingredients	12-15 portions	Method
Yeast	½ oz.	Dissolve yeast in milk.
Milk, scalded, cooled	3 oz.	
Sugar	4 oz.	Add; mix well.
Salt	½ oz.	
Lemon juice	1 Tbsp.	
Vanilla	1 Tbsp.	
Flour	1 lb.	Add.
Butter, melted	4 oz.	Add; let dough rise about 30 minutes, then roll and put on a greased sheet pan. Reserve in cool place.
Sugar	5 oz.	Combine; heat to boiling.
Butter	5 oz.	
Honey	1 tsp.	
Cream	1 tsp.	
Almonds, ground fine	7½ oz.	Add; spread hot mixture over yeast dough. Let rise. Bake at 380F until bottom and top are brown. Let cool.
Prepared custard	as needed	Slice in 2 layers; fill with custard. Reassemble layers.

Flaming Fresh Strawberries   (A. Wisnesky)

Ingredients	8 portions	Method
Fresh strawberries	2 pt.	Wash and hull.
Butter	4 oz.	Slowly heat in saucepan until carmelized.
Sugar	6 oz.	
Orange juice, fresh	6 oz.	Add; simmer until mixture is smooth. Add strawberries; cook for 3½ minutes.
Orange-flavored liqueur	2 oz.	
Cognac	2 oz.	Pour over strawberries; ignite. Pour over ice cream.

Carolina Ice Cream Pie   (A. Ausserlechner)

Ingredients	6-8 portions	Method
Butter, melted	4 oz.	Combine; line a 10-in. pie pan. Refrigerate.
Sugar	1 oz.	
Graham cracker crumbs	2½ oz.	
Vanilla ice cream, softened	1½ pt.	Fill pie shell until smooth and even. Freeze for 1 hour.
Egg whites	3	Place in copper bowl.
Lemon, juice of	¼	Add; beat with whisk until stiff peaks form.
Sugar	3 oz.	
Vanilla	dash	Add; transfer to piping bag and working quickly, pipe rosettes to totally cover pie surface. Brown under broiler. Refreeze.

Best Cake (F. Sgro)

Ingredients	8 portions	Method
Eggs	2	Mix with wooden spoon to blend. Grease and flour a 9 x 13-in pan. Pour in mixture; bake at 350F for 35-40 minutes; cool at room temperature.
Flour	2 cups	
Sugar	2 cups	
Baking soda	2 tsp.	
Vanilla	1 tsp.	
Nuts, chopped	½-1 cup	
Canned crushed pineapple, juice included	20 oz.	
Cream cheese	8 oz.	Blend in mixer; spread over cake.
Margarine	8 oz.	
Confectioners' sugar	1 cup	
Vanilla extract	1 tsp.	

Bread Pudding and Hot Whiskey Sauce (F. Mahnke)

Ingredients	4 portions	Method
French bread slices, ½-in. thick	5	Butter each slice French bread; arrange in 2-qt. baking dish, buttered side up.
Butter	3 Tbsp.	
Eggs	3	Beat together.
Sugar	½ cup	
Black rum	1 oz.	
Milk	2 cups	Combine in saucepan; heat to boiling. Combine with egg mixture; strain over bread. Bake in waterbath at 375F for 45 minutes.
Heavy cream	½ cup	
Vanilla extract	½ tsp.	
Milk	1 qt.	Scald.
Egg yolks	6	Whip together; combine with hot milk. Simmer but do not boil for 5 minutes. Serve over bread pudding.
Bourbon	¼ cup	
Sugar	½ cup	
Cornstarch	1 tsp.	

Soufflé Orange (F. Nikodemus)

Ingredients	10-12 portions	Method
Butter, melted	4 oz.	Combine.
Flour	3 oz.	
Milk	11 oz.	Heat milk to boiling; add salt, lemon and orange rind. Add butter and flour; mix. Cool for 1 minute.
Salt	pinch	
Lemon rind, grated	½ tsp.	
Orange rind, grated	1 Tbsp.	
Orange-flavored liqueur	4 oz.	Add.
Egg yolks	10	Add; stir over heat until blended. Prepare soufflé dish by brushing lightly with butter and dusting with sugar.
Egg whites	10	Beat in a very clean bowl.
Sugar	6½ oz.	Add when egg whites begin to form stiff peaks. Fold into orange mixture. Fill soufflé dish three-quarters full. Bake at 375F for 20 minutes.

Sabayon Au Chocolat

(B. Bardy)

Ingredients	6 portions	Method
Egg yolks	12	Combine.
Dry sherry	⅓ cup	
Kirschwasser	2 Tbsp.	
Vanilla extract	½ tsp.	
Salt	pinch	Add. Place over double boiler; beat steadily in same direction. When mixture becomes thick and fluffy, remove from heat. Continue beating until bowl cools.
Nutmeg	pinch	
Confectioners' sugar	¾ cup	
Milk chocolate chips, melted	1½ cups	Fold in. Place in dessert glasses and serve hot or chilled.

Shortcake

(D. Gee)

Ingredients	24 portions	Method
Flour	13 oz.	Combine; mix well.
Salt	¼ oz.	
Baking powder	¾ oz.	
Sugar	1½ oz.	
Shortening	2½ oz.	Cut or rub in.
Milk	1 cup	Fold in. Roll out dough to ½-in. thick; cut with biscuit cutter. Place on buttered pan. Let rest a few minutes; bake at 375F until done. Reserve.
Egg	1	
Sugar	2 lb., 4 oz.	Combine in saucepan; heat to boiling.
Water	1 qt.	
Salt	¼ oz.	
Gelatin	1 oz.	
Cornstarch	1½ oz.	
Butter	2 oz.	
Canned apricot purée	8 oz.	
Water	1 cup	Add water, sugar and agar; heat to boiling. Let cool; add food coloring.
Sugar	4 oz.	
Agar	1 oz.	
Red food coloring	3 drops	
Strawberries, sliced	as needed	Put biscuits in individual dishes; top with sliced strawberries. Put glaze over biscuit and strawberries with small ladle.

Lime Pie

(K. Sehl)

Ingredients	8 portions	Method
Egg yolks	3	Beat until pale yellow.
Sweetened condensed milk	16 oz.	Blend in.
Lime juice	½ cup	Add slowly. Pour into pie shell. Bake at 360F for 10 minutes; cool at room temperature.
Lime, zest of	1	
Whipping cream	1 cup	Whip to a soft peak.
Confectioners' sugar	⅓ cup	Add; whip until stiff. Top pie.

Chef Eid's Delight Cookies With Lemon   (K. Eid)

Ingredients	6 dozen	Method
Sugar	10 oz.	Combine; mix at low speed until sugar is incorpo-
Shortening	1 lb.	rated.
Butter	4 oz.	
Eggs	5	Add eggs and some of the flour to prevent cur-
Cake flour	1 lb., 4 oz.	dling.
Lemon pudding mix	10 oz.	Add with rest of flour until mixture is completely
Salt	pinch	absorbed in flour.
Lemon flavoring	1 Tbsp.	Add; refrigerate for several hours. Scale off dough in
Yellow food coloring	3 drops	10 oz. portions; make a roll 1½-in. in diameter and 8-in. long. Shape oval; cool again until stiff.
Egg whites	as needed	Brush dough with egg whites; roll in yellow sugar.
Yellow granulated sugar	as needed	Cut into ⅛-in. thick ovals; place on paper-lined pan. Bake at 390F for 10 minutes.
Lemon fondant	2 oz.	Put a dot in middle of each oval while still warm; remove when cold.

Brown Bread Ice Cream   (R. Nelson)

Ingredients	6 portions	Method
Brown bread crumbs	3 cups	Spread on baking tray. Toast in 375-400F oven until crisp and brown; reserve.
Whipping cream	1½ cups	Combine; whip.
Light cream	1 cup	
Light brown sugar	1 cup	Beat in.
Egg yolks	2	Mix together; add to cream mixture. Beat in well.
Rum	1 Tbsp.	Fold crumbs gently into whipped cream mixture.
Egg whites	2	Whip until stiff; fold into cream-crumb mixture. Freeze. Makes approximately 1½-2 qt.

Molasses Cookies   (S. Nicas)

Ingredients	6 dozen	Method
Sugar	2 lb.	Combine; mix well.
Shortening	1 lb.	
Molasses	2½ lb.	
Corn syrup	½ lb.	
Salt	1½ oz.	
Baking powder	2 oz.	
Milk, powdered	2 oz.	
Ginger	½ oz.	
Eggs	8 oz.	Add.
Water	20 oz.	Add.
Pastry flour	3½ lb.	Add; beat until dough forms. Roll out to ¼-in.
Bread flour	2½ lb.	thickness; cut with 3-in. cookie cutter. Bake at 390-400F for 15 minutes.

State of Maine Baked Indian Pudding

(F. Lozier)

Ingredients	12 portions	Method
Milk	1 qt.	Scald in heavy saucepan.
Molasses Cornmeal	½ cup ⅓ cup	Combine; add to hot milk. Heat to boiling.
Sugar Salt Cinnamon Ginger	1 cup ½ tsp. ½ tsp. ½ tsp.	Combine.
Eggs, beaten	2	Add sugar mixture to eggs.
Butter, melted	1 Tbsp.	Add. Add sugar mixture to milk mixture; return to a good boil. Pour hot mixture into a buttered baking pan, about 8 x 8-in. Bake at 300F for 30 minutes.
Milk	⅔ cup	Stir in; continue baking for another 1½ hours. Cool completely in refrigerator and reheat as needed. Serve very hot with a small scoop of vanilla ice cream placed in each serving or with whipped cream.

Banana Cheese Cake

(E. Newman)

Ingredients	12 portions	Method
Graham cracker crumbs Confectioners' sugar Butter, melted Orange rind, grated	1½ cups ⅓ cup 6 oz. ¼ tsp.	Combine; press into bottom and sides of 9-in. lightly greased springform pan.
Butterscotch pudding mix	4 oz.	Mix half package with ½ amount of milk called for. Heat until slightly thickened and bubbly. Remove from heat; cover with plastic wrap; cool.
Cream cheese	24 oz.	Beat until fluffy.
Medium eggs	3	Add; beat until blended.
Cornstarch	1 tsp.	Add.
Confectioners' sugar Vanilla extract Maple extract Banana-flavored liqueur Large bananas, mashed	¾ cup ½ tsp. ½ tsp. 2 oz. 2	Mix in with remaining pudding. Pour into prepared pan. Bake at 375F for 50 minutes or until knife inserted in center comes out clean.
Sour cream Sugar Egg yolks	1 cup ¼ cup 2	Combine; spread over cake. Return to oven for 10 minutes. Garnish with sliced bananas; glaze with heated apricot jelly.

GLOSSARY OF CULINARY TERMS

A la According to the style of, such as a la Francaise or according to the French way.

À la carte Food prepared to order. Each dish priced separately.

Aspic A flavored jellylike substance, made from meat, fish, poultry, game or vegetables, stock or fruit juice to which gelatin has been added. It is used to coat all of the above named items or to form molds.

Au jus Meat served with only the natural unthickened pan juices.

Baste To ladle pan drippings, wine or other liquid over meat, while roasting, to hold in moisture and flavor.

Batter A mixture of flour, sugar, eggs, milk and seasonings. Its consistancy may range from a thin liquid to a stiff thick one, depending on the proportions of the ingredients.

Beurre Manié Butter thickened with flour and used for sauces.

Buerre Noir Browned butter.

Blanch To plunge into boiling water for the purpose of softening food, removing unwanted flavor or partial precooking or to facilitate the removal of skins from tomatoes, nuts or fruits.

Bind To thicken or smooth the consistency of a liquid. Egg yolks, flour, potatoes or rice are commonly used.

Bouillon A liquid resulting from the simmering of flesh and bones of meat or fish with vegetables, water and seasoning.

Bouquet Garni A bunch of herbs tied together as a bouquet or put in a cheesecloth bag for the purpose of seasoning a cooked item.

Bread To pass an item through flour, beaten eggs and bread crumbs.

Brunoise Vegetables diced into small pieces to be used to garnish soups and sauces.

Cheesecloth A lightweight cotton fabric with an extremely loose weave used for straining soups and sauces.

Clarify To make a substance pure or clear.

Clarified Butter Purified butterfat, with water and milk solids removed.

Consommé A clear, strong-flavored stock.

Court Bouillon A liquid comprised of water and vinegar or wine or lemon juice, usually flavored with root and stock, with vegetables, seasonings and herbs added. It is used to cook fish, vegetables and a variety of meats.

Crêpe A thin pancake. Crêpes may be filled, rolled and baked for an entree. Sweet crêpes are served as a dessert with confectioners sugar or with a sauce.

Deglaze Adding water, wine, stock or cream to a pan in which meats have been roasted or sautéed to dissolve crusted juices that have dried on the bottom of the pan. Used as a base for sauces.

Degrease To remove fat from hot liquid. Let liquid stand for awhile; skim the surface with a ladle. When liquid is refrigerated, fat congeals on the surface and can be easily removed.

Demiglaze A rich brown sauce that has been reduced by half.

Devein Remove the vein running along a shrimp's or lobster's back. With a small knife, make a shallow cut along the vein and scrape or lift out the cavity.

Dice To cut into small even cubes.

Dilute Add liquid to another substance in order to thin or weaken it.

Dredge To coat an item with dry ingredients, usually flour.

Dust To sprinkle the surface of food lightly with sugar, flour or crumbs.

Egg wash Egg yolk diluted with water, milk or cream. Used to give color and gloss to yeast dough and puff pastry.

Emulsion A liquid mixture suspended in another (eggs and oil) to prevent separation.

Espagnole A sauce made of brown stock and flavoring ingredients and thickened with a brown roux.

Farce A mixture of meat, poultry, fish or vegetables used for stuffing.

Flambé To flavor food with an alcohol by igniting the liquid. The alcohol burns off, but the flavor remains.

Fillet A piece or slice of boneless, lean meat or fish.

Fricassée A white stew in which the meat is cooked in fat without browning, before liquid is added.

Fumet A flavorful stock, usually fish stock.

Glace de Viande Meat glaze; a reduction of brown stock.

Glaze 1) A stock that is reduced until it coats the back of a spoon; 2) a shiny coating, such as a syrup, applied to a food; or 3) to make a food shiny or glossy by coating it with a glaze or by browning under a broiler or in a hot oven.

Grill To cook meat or fish on a gridiron over hot coals. The term is used interchangeably with broil.

Hors d'ouevre Small appetizers or canapes served before a meal or as a first course of meal. They may be served in many forms either hot or cold.

Julienne Meat or vegetables cut into fine strips.

Liaison A thickening and binding agent usually beaten egg yolks and cream or blood, used in the preparation of soups and sauces.

Marinate To soak a food in a seasoned liquid.

Mince To chop into very fine pieces.

Mirepoix A mixture a vegetables, generally rough cut. Used as a flavoring for meats, stuffings, stews and sauces.

Mornay sauce Bechamel sauce thickened with a liaison and flavored with grated cheese.

Poaching Cooking eggs, fish in liquid that is just barely brought to a simmer.

Reduce To evaporate a liquid rapidly to a required concentration to intensify its flavor.

Roux The roux is the thickening element is a sauce, usually made from butter and flour.

Salamander Small broiler used primarily for browning or glazing the tops of certain food items.

Shallots Onionlike plant with clustered bulbs that resemble garlic but are milder. Used for seasoning soups and sauces.

Sauté A primary cooking technique to brown or cook food in very hot oil, in a shallow pan.

Simmer To cook a liquid barely to a boiling point. The surface should show only a few bubbles breaking slowly.

Skim Using a skimmer or ladle to remove scum or grease accumulated on top of a soup, stock or sauce.

Stock A clear, thin liquid flavored by soluble substances extracted from meat, poultry and fish and their bones, and from vegetables and seasonings.

Sweat To cook in a small amount of fat over low heat, sometimes covered.

Thicken To make a liquid mixture more dense by adding an agent like cornstarch, flour, egg yolks, rice or potatoes.

Toss To cause a rising and falling action for the purpose of blending certain ingredients together such as various types of salads.

Tournedos A small beef steak cut from the tenderloin.

Velouté A basic white sauce made from a roux of butter and flour to which stock from poultry, veal or fish is added.

Whip To beat rapidly to increase the volume and incorporate air.

Zest Pieces of peel or of thin oily outer skin of citrus fruits used to flavor.

INDEX

INDEX